Value Investing
Made Easy

Books by Janet Lowe

Dividends Don't Lie: Finding Value in Blue-Chip Stocks
  with Geraldine Weiss

*Benjamin Graham on Value Investing: Lessons from the Dean of Wall
  Street*

The Super Saver: Fundamental Strategies for Building Wealth

Keys to Investing in International Stocks

The Secret Empire: How 25 Multi-Nationals Rule the World

Value Investing Made Easy

Janet Lowe

McGRAW-HILL
New York • San Francisco • Washington, D.C. • Auckland • Bogotá
Caracas • Lisbon • London • Madrid • Mexico City • Milan
Montreal • New Delhi • San Juan • Singapore
Sydney • Tokyo • Toronto

Library of Congress Cataloging-in-Publication Data

Lowe, Janet.
    Value investing made easy / by Janet Lowe
        p.   cm.
    Includes bibliographical references and index.
    ISBN 0-07-038859-8 (HC)   ISBN 0-07-038864-4 (PBK)
    1. Investment analysis.   2. Securities—United States.   I. Title.
HG4529.L68   1996
332.6—dc20   96-12418
                                                          CIP

McGraw-Hill

A Division of The McGraw·Hill Companies

    567890 DOC/DOC   02

ISBN 0-07-038859-8 (HC)
ISBN 0-07-038864-4 (PBK)

The sponsoring editor for this book was *David Conti*, the editing supervisor
was *Patricia V. Amoroso*, and the production supervisor was *Donald F. Schmidt*.
It was designed and set in Galliard by *TopDesk Publishers' Group*.

Printed and bound by R. R. Donnelly & Sons Company.

This publication is designed to provide accurate and authoritative information in
regard to the subject matter covered. It is sold with the understanding that the
publisher is not engaged in rendering legal, accounting, or other professional
service. If legal advice of other expert assistance is required, the services of a
competent professional person should be sought.
    *—From a declaration of principles jointly adopted by a committee
    of the American Bar Association and a committee of publishers.*

This book is printed on recycled, acid-free paper containing a
minimum of 50% recycled, de-inked fiber.

To Warren H. Buffett, with appreciation for his encouragement, help, and inspiration.

CONTENTS

Foreword

Successful investors, like successful doctors, must have a good understanding of the hard facts expressed in numbers—but then these must be applied properly to real-life cases. If the art of investing were actually easy, or quickly achieved, no one would be in the lower or middle classes.

Nevertheless, there are many lessons to be learned and to be a successful investor learning is essential. Security prices are as volatile as ocean waves—they range from calm to stormy. Shrewd investors must estimate what the possible financial climate is and is likely to become. They must resist following the crowd; when everyone is making money these investors know this portends a decline.

The current extended rising markets recall those of 1929 and 1968. Rising markets attract noninvestors to join the game of speculation with borrowed money or reduced margins. Today, low-priced options become substitutes for the higher priced actual issues. The public is spellbound by daily price moves. Less noticed are long-term economic changes that ultimately set future prices.

The current bull market has caused over 6,000 mutual funds to be formed so there is a wide choice by type and size. Most are run by younger managers with limited experience of past major changes in price cycles. The inconsistent results of most money managers over most annual periods is evidence of how unreliable it is to predict the general market.

Value investing, an approach that I had the opportunity to study in detail while I served as Benjamin Graham's classroom teaching assistant at Columbia University from 1931 to 1956, is one of the best ways to step apart from the crowd and to protect oneself from the unpredictable behavior of the securities markets. I have long followed the principles taught by Graham at my own New York investment management firm, Kahn Bros.

Most readers know someone who has had a successful career of investing profitably—search that person out. If your capital can afford it, be guided by a reputable money manager with several years, not a weekly, time horizon. Avoid believing self-serving, bullish corporate publicity. Stock repurchases by management may, for example, prove to be bearish.

The author's wide-ranging contact with many of America's most successful investors makes understandable their management styles in simple and usable terms. Janet Lowe supplies extensive sources to tap for guidance, especially on how to avoid over-valued stocks.

Between the ultra depression-conservatism of Ben Graham and the brilliance of monopoly investor Warren Buffett, there are ample levels that should fit your own pattern of risk to reward, suitable for your capital needs and lifestyle.

Value Investing Made Easy is both solidly researched and clearly written. New investors will find a wide range of definitions and directions to make their savings more likely to grow than wither. When specific investment choices become difficult, rereading Lowe's book should save you from decisions that diminish your capital.

Irving Kahn, CFA

Preface

When *Benjamin Graham on Value Investing: Lessons from the Dean of Wall Street* was published in 1994, readers often asked if by chance I had intended a "Graham and Dodd made easy" book. They were referring to Benjamin Graham and David Dodd, the authors of *Security Analysis*. That was not the book I had written. Rather, I had told the story of Graham, the driving force behind the professional advancement of security analysis, his dramatic life, and how his investment philosophy evolved.

By coming back again and again with intelligent questions, readers made it clear that they wanted to learn even more about Graham's principles, the combined work of Graham and Dodd, and the fundamentals of value investing. On top of that, they wanted the information in an easy-to-digest form. They were looking for *Value Investing Made Easy*.

Graham and Dodd's authoritative text, still called the "bible" of security analysis, was first written in 1934. Graham's second classic, *The Intelligent Investor*, was published in 1954. Subsequent editions of both books are still found on bookstore and library shelves, and I recommend them highly.

Despite an impressive publishing record, Graham sometimes referred to his own books as ones most often quoted and least read by investors. That statement was partly based on modesty. Even now Graham and Dodd enjoy a loyal following. Nevertheless, today's investors may be reluctant to plunge into Graham and Dodd. Life is so busy that many investors hesitate before picking up an 850-page volume to read. And the challenges today are different. The size of the market has exploded and industrial dynamics have shifted. The NAS-DAQ, created to be a market for smaller companies, has seized an ever more prominent role in the investment world. The securities of international corporations and foreign nations have more and more of a place in portfolios of individual investors.

The competition for investors' attention is intense and, last but not least, our wish for a personal portfolio that will outperform those of our relatives, neighbors, and coworkers is extraordinary.

While investors, both individual and professional, still love and respect Graham and Dodd, they may be unsure of how to adapt their doctrines to the twenty-first century. It is the goal of this book to present the foundations of value investing in simple language, and to show how those principles still apply both today and in the coming millennium. To do so, I've commandeered some of the writing and teaching techniques that Graham and Dodd used so successfully.

Warren Buffett, Walter Schloss, Irving Kahn, and others who studied with Benjamin Graham at Columbia University and the New York Institute of Finance say that his teachings were real and relevant because Graham cited current examples. In fact, his case studies often related to situations existing on the stock exchange the very day of class. His lessons could be applied immediately, and quite often his students went to work the next day and executed trades on the basis of lessons learned the night before.

I've adopted some of Graham's teaching devices in this book. True stories of actual companies are used to show how a concept works. As a result, it becomes clear that the principles of value investing remain valid. That's what this book is—a guide to value investing as originally taught by Ben Graham and David Dodd and subsequently practiced and improved upon by dozens of remarkable investors.

Here is what the book is *not* about: This book is not an academic treatise pitting various investment principles against one another. I will present the argument in favor of value investing in the beginning in simple terms. The track records of dedicated value investors are proof enough. Those who are not convinced can pursue the debate in greater depth elsewhere.

In the past the "efficient market" hypothesis and "random walk" theory were seen as evidence that value investing has no merit. I've seen the television shows in which a chimpanzee is pitted against an investment expert. In the few short weeks the television camera crew is willing to track the results, perhaps a chimpanzee could do better. Admittedly, some so-called investment experts are not much better than a chimpanzee. But so far, I know of no successful, affluent investor who is willing to turn an investment portfolio over to a dart-throwing chimp. The very fact that so many people place their money in the hands of professional managers is some indication that practical people, despite academic studies, reject the "efficient market," the "random walk," and similar theories. In recent years academic research has discounted those theories, giving credence to common sense.

This book is written for both the professional and the individual investor. But I'd like to send a special message to investors who fear that value investing is too technical for them to grasp.

While writing this book I met a businesswoman whose hobby is horseback riding. A lifelong student and practitioner of English saddle, she loves leading her horse over high fences. When she learned that I write about investments, she became very interested. "I'm afraid to buy stocks. What if the price goes down and I lose my money?" she said, then added, "Of course, I have a broker whom I trust and he helps me make decisions."

The last sentence wasn't said with much conviction. As we talked further, I realized that what bothered her was not her broker's skill, but her own lack of knowledge. "I watch *Wall Street Week* on television. These people are experts, and they're so often wrong. My broker is honest, but he could be wrong too," she said. I suggested that she would trust her broker more if she were better equipped to judge his performance.

"How would a novice rider feel if she attempted to leap a 4-foot barrier astride a spirited pony?" I asked.

"She'd be terrified, and she very likely would get dumped, and maybe even get hurt," responded the woman.

While I don't want to imply that securities and horses have much in common, some lessons are transferable. Ignorance increases the chances of getting dumped. Too little knowledge makes all of us nervous, suspicious, and ultimately resentful if something goes wrong.

When buying a house or a car or consulting a doctor, we try to learn as much as we can about the whole process in order to participate in decisions and decide for ourselves whether the advice given seems appropriate. Our homes and our health are so important that we must take personal responsibility and participate in decisions.

Likewise, our money is too important to simply abandon personal responsibility to someone else, no matter how knowledgeable or honest that person is. If my friend has the courage and skill to ride a horse over a high white fence, she certainly can grasp the principles of value investing. With training and practice, she would even enjoy the experience. Investing, just like horseback riding, can be risky. But the more you know, the lower the risk. And the more you know, the greater the pleasure.

She and other readers will find that the teachings of Ben Graham can be stated in simple language, but they carry a profound message. Anyone can understand the precepts and everyone can profit from them. The goal of this book is to simplify some of the teachings of Graham and Dodd. "We have striven throughout to guard the student against overemphasis upon the superficial and the temporary," the authors wrote in the preface to the first edition of *Security Analysis*. That purpose remains unchanged in *Value Investing Made Easy*.

At intervals in *Value Investing Made Easy* the reader will find this icon:

Following these sturdy pillars will be a quotation. These are relevant words from Graham, widely recognized as the father of value investing. In cases indicated by the footnote, the quote may come from Graham and Dodd's *Security Analysis*.

It is not my intention to replace or update the work of Graham and Dodd, or books Graham wrote on his own. With some preparation, perhaps the timid reader will feel better approaching *The Intelligent Investor* and *Security Analysis*. I hope so. It will be a unique and enlightening experience.

A few comments and suggestions before you begin reading.

To some, the value investing principles espoused here may seem to ignore the moral, ethical, and philosophical aspects of the business world. *Value Investing Made Easy* is dedicated to the quantitative and qualitative aspects of investing, but the fact that ethics in investing is not addressed does not diminish the importance of this subject. Ethical investing is compatible with and can be effectively integrated into value principles. All investors should be able to find value stocks that are compatible with their belief systems.

At the end of this book are two important segments. Many readers will want to review the glossary before beginning the book. Some of the terminology may be new and may even verge on jargon. Though every effort was made to avoid obscure or overly complicated language, it's sometimes unavoidable. The glossary is intended to defeat the hidden agenda of those who toss out jargon—to exclude newcomers from the inner circle of understanding.

Also included is a reading list of books that I've found both educational and entertaining. (In fact, I wrote a couple of them myself!) The more you read about investing, the better off you will be, since no single book contains all the wisdom necessary to manage investments well. A primary source of research for this book was Graham and Dodd's *Security Analysis*, though not the most recent edition. Readers will need to keep in mind that when Graham and Dodd are quoted, most often the quote comes from the 1940 edition. This was the last edition that the two Columbia professors wrote almost entirely on their own and quite purely reflects their thinking. I have tried to acknowledge and make allowances for the way times have changed in 56 years.

Finally, many thanks to all those who helped make this book possible. Thanks to Austin Lynas for his editing and research assistance; to my literary agent Alice Fried Martell; to my editor David Conti; and to Warren Buffett, Charles Brandes, Arthur Q. Johnson, Frank K. Martin, Jerry Ringer, and many others.

The Virtue of Value Investing

It baffles us how many people know of Ben Graham but so few follow. We tell our principles freely and write about them extensively in our annual reports. They are easy to learn. They should be easy to follow. But the only thing anyone wants to know is, "What are we buying today?" Like Graham, we are widely recognized but the least followed.[1]

WARREN BUFFETT

O maha billionaire investor Warren Buffett made this observation at the 1995 annual meeting of Berkshire Hathaway Inc., just months before he collected $2.1 billion (pretax) on the sale of Capital Cities/ABC to the Walt Disney Co., thus ensuring another spectacular annual return for his holding company. Buffett often pays homage to his late teacher, mentor, former employer, and friend, Benjamin Graham.

It mystifies Buffett that the majority of investors pursue and adopt one Wall Street fad after another when the secret to safety and high returns is right under their noses and has been for many decades. The humble principles of value investing have been in use since the early 1900s, and they've allowed investors to survive and prosper in the great bull and bear markets of this century. Graham walked his investment strategies through the most stringent real-life investment test ever—the Crash of 1929.

Though Graham is known as the father of value investing, when he first started teaching investment principles at Columbia University, Graham put no particular name on his concepts. His goal was simply to present a logical, reality-based approach to investing. When Graham and his coauthor David Dodd wrote the influential *Security Analysis* in 1934, their intention was the same. The book became a classic. It has been the beacon by which many brilliant investors were guided.

VALUE INVESTING IN A NUTSHELL

A value investor buys shares in a company as though he were buying the whole company, paying little attention to stock market temperament, the political climate or other exterior conditions.

As simple as it may sound, the value investor buys a stock as if he were buying the corner store. In the process he might ask himself a series of questions. Is the business on sound financial footing? Will I be assuming large debt? Does the price include the building and land? Will it generate a steady, strong income stream? What kind of return on my investment will it produce? Is there potential for sales and income growth?

If the investor comes up with the right answers, and if he can buy the store for less than its actual future worth to the buyer, then he has found a bargain. He's discovered a value investment.

This is a simplification, of course. A mom-and-pop shop is easier to understand than a global industrial conglomerate such as Unilever, DuPont, or Daimler Benz.

During a speech late in his life Graham described his investment approach in his own words. His message? Concern yourself only with those things that matter:

> My reputation—such as it is, or perhaps as recently revived—seems to be associated chiefly with the concept of "value." But I have been truly interested solely in such aspects of value as present themselves in a clear and convincing manner, derived from the basic elements of earning power and balance-sheet position, with no emphasis at all placed on such matters as small variations in the growth rate from quarter to quarter, or the inclusion or exclusion of minor items in calculating the so-called "primary earnings." Most significant here, I have resolutely turned my back on efforts to predict the future.[2]

BUILD FROM THE BASE

Investors today may recognize value investing by one of its currently popular synonyms—bottom-up investing. Seth Klarman, a high-achieving investment manager from Boston who applies many of Graham's principles, has been described as a bottom-up or "small picture" investor.

James Grant, publisher of the biweekly newsletter *Grant's Interest Rate Observer*, describes Klarman this way: "If he has views on Gorbachev, the German bond market, the business cycle, or the global yield curve, he does not call his broker because of them. He does not talk about 'support' or 'resistance,' and he might worry as little about the Federal Reserve system as any white-collar worker in the greater Boston area. He invests from the 'bottom up,' as he says, not the 'top down'—'I buy individual values.'"[3]

Klarman says, "Top-down people would spend a whole lot of time looking at how bad the economy might get or how many sellers there might be. Bottom-up value investors basically look at the values they buy. They leave room to average down, but they buy if they think the values are compelling."[4]

James Grant is such a devotee of Graham that he named his book *Minding Mr. Market* after a parable Graham often used in his Columbia University classes. We'll meet the addled Mr. Market in Chapter 7.

VALUE INVESTING SUPERSTARS

Though value investors such as Buffett and Klarman are well known and their records are impressive, Andrew Bary pointed out in a 1995 *Barron's* profile of 90-plus-year-old securities analyst Irving Kahn that "the world of strict value investors on Wall Street these days is quite small."[5] Nevertheless, the gospel of value investing is still sermonized, and to their everlasting reward, some of the most successful investors of all time have been disciples of Benjamin Graham.

In his now-famous 1976 eulogy to Graham at Columbia University, Buffett described one elite group of value seekers as "The Superinvestors of Graham and Doddsville." Buffett himself often wears the crown of the richest man in the nation. (Whether or not he beats out Microsoft's Bill Gates for first place each year depends on small variations in large numbers.) Buffett's Berkshire Hathaway has a market value of more than $25 billion and is infamous for its five figure stock price, taking up multiple lines on the New York Stock Exchange newspaper listings. Buffett has doggedly given investors a 28.6 percent

COMPARISON OF INVESTMENT PERFORMANCE

TYPE OF INVESTOR	PERIOD	RATE OF RETURN (%)
Warren Buffet—growth-oriented value investor	1957–1994	28.6
Kahn Brothers—capital preservation value investors	1990–1994	19.3
Growth-oriented mutual funds	5 years ending 8/1/95	15.36
Global mutual funds	5 years ending 8/1/95	10.73
Standard & Poor's	5 years ending 9/30/95	17.24

return on their investment year in and year out for 30 years. The annual return on the Standard & Poor's 500 was a laggard 10 percent.

Less of a pop culture hero than Buffett, but nevertheless well known in financial circles, is Irving Kahn, founder of the New York firm of Kahn Brothers. A long-time associate of Benjamin Graham, Kahn and his sons quietly manage $250 million in securities. Every year from 1990 to 1994, the value of Kahn Brothers' stock portfolio rose an average of 19.3 percent.

In addition to Kahn and his sons, other remarkably dependable and thriving value investment firms include Tweedy Browne; the phenomenally successful Sequoia Fund; Walter and Edwin Schloss Associates; California-based Brandes Investment Partners; Canada's Peter Cundill & Associates; and Quest Advisors, operators of the Pennsylvania Mutual Fund. Their lifelong annual returns range between 13 and 20 percent. Clearly, growth and global funds are not the only place to be for long-term gains.

THE MASTERS' VOICES

It is no accident that *Value Investing Made Easy* relies heavily on the words and wisdom of many of these contemporary value investors, Warren Buffett in particular. If Benjamin Graham is the chief gardener in the orchard garden of safety and value investment, Buffett is the gardener's apprentice with the greenest thumb. Those who were classmates with Buffett when he studied under Graham at Columbia say that the two men, despite their age difference, were remarkable matches of intellect, temperament, and ethics. They both loved jokes, even corny ones. Yet Buffett is not a slavish follower of Graham; he has, in fact, tinkered with and fine-tuned Graham's technology.

The many ways of applying value investing principles were demonstrated at a memorial celebrating the hundredth year of Graham's birth. The event was held at the New York Society of Securities Analysts in January 1995. Walter Schloss and Warren Buffett both were among the speakers. Buffett described his own virtually permanent core portfolio, and his preference for a small number of superior stocks.

"If you understand a business," Buffett said, "you don't need very many of them." However, he added, Schloss had also followed the value principles and made a fortune buying a large number of very cheap stocks. "It is what I call the used cigar butt approach, where the cigars you find are well smoked, down to the nub. But they're free. You pick the butt up and get one good puff. Anything is a buy at a price," Buffett said.

This is not heresy. Despite their devotion to his ideals, most of Graham's apostles do find their own variations on the theme, as Graham perhaps expected they would. Graham was not an iconoclast. Though for nearly 50 years he was one of America's most respected investment managers, Graham regularly retested his theories and experimented with modifications. Even when he had reached his eighties, he put aside an hour every day to study stocks and their performances, continually digging for a simpler and even more straightforward way to achieve superior investment results.

BENJAMIN GRAHAM

After Benjamin Graham's death in 1976, the *Financial Analysts Journal* published a eulogy in which Warren Buffett described Graham's active mind. "Virtually total recall, unending fascination with new knowledge, and an ability to recast it in a form applicable to seemingly unrelated problems made exposure to his thinking in any field a delight," wrote Buffett.[6] A charismatic man but one of great personal reserve, Graham was a successful investor, writer, and professor. Founder of the New York investment firm of Graham Newman, he also was the driving force behind the establish-

(Graham con't)
ment of professional training, testing, and certification for financial analysts.

Graham was born in London in 1894, and was an infant when his parents immigrated to New York. Soon afterward his father died, leaving his mother to raise three sons. Graham grew up in trying financial circumstances, but because of his exceptional intelligence he won a scholarship to Columbia University. Though Graham had excelled at classic languages, mathematics, and philosophy, his dean arranged for him to join a New York investment firm upon graduation. Graham knew nothing about Wall Street when he reported to work there in 1914.

No sooner had Graham started than World War I forced the New York markets to go dark. When they reopened, Graham quickly showed skill in picking up the ways of the Street and devising ingenious new approaches to investing. Soon he was managing money for others. By the 1920s Graham was fabulously successful and full of self-confidence. But again, his fortunes reversed.

The Crash of 1929 ravaged not only Graham's investment portfolio but also his plan to write a book on his investment principles. Despite his skills and dedication, Graham's clients lost money along with everyone else. Graham

and his partner, Jerome Newman, worked 5 years without compensation until their clients' fortunes were fully restored. Though the experience was dreadful, it earned Graham widespread respect for his integrity as a money manager.

In 1934, just as investors had given up on the stock market, Graham and coauthor David Dodd published the acclaimed *Security Analysis*. Dodd, a bright new professor, had been enlisted to take notes as Graham lectured at Columbia. Those notes became the basis for *Security Analysis*. Updated numerous times, the book is the longest running investment text ever published and is available today. Dedicated investors call it their "bible."

Early editions of Graham and Dodd are valued by collectors and sell for premium prices. Those early editions make engrossing reading because they show how much things change and how much they don't. For example, the authors describe pyramids, Ponzis, penny stock frauds and other schemes that are just as common today as they ever were. Their analyses of legitimate, but nevertheless problematic investment decisions also are eerily contemporary. They use actual companies—General Electric, Ford Motor Co., and Archer Daniels Midland, to name a few—to illustrate important points.

In 1949 Graham wrote *The*

(Graham con't)
Intelligent Investor for the non-professional investor. That book has been revised several times and is still found on most bookstore shelves today.

Once the Graham Newman Co. recouped its portfolio of 1929–30, Graham never again lost money for his clients. Over a 30-year period—through the Crash of 1929, the Great Depression, and two world wars—Graham's clients earned an average annual return of about 17 percent, and that did not include their earnings on Geico.

In 1948 Graham bought the then privately held Government Employees Insurance Co. (Geico) for his portfolio without realizing that an investment fund could not own an insurance company. He disposed of the acquisition by taking the company public and distributing its shares to Graham Newman fund holders. The share price immediately skyrocketed. Though the return that individual shareholders made on Geico is impossible to calculate, since it depends on when their stock was sold, by 1972 the shares had appreciated more than 28,000 percent. In many cases, Geico shares have been held within the original families, with ownership passing from one generation to the next. Geico's history as a value play came full circle in 1995 when

Buffett bought the remaining 49 percent of the company that he didn't already own. (See the Appendix for the full Geico story.)

Graham once remarked that before the Geico investment, Graham and Newman were considered good financial analysts; afterward they were considered geniuses.

Graham taught a 2-hour course once a week at Columbia University from 1928 until his retirement in 1956. In January of 1929 the class was so popular that 150 students signed up. Even after the crash his seminars were fully enrolled and were instrumental in helping build Columbia's reputation as a business school. It was at Columbia that young Warren Buffett emerged as Graham's stellar student. Buffett later persuaded Graham to let him go to work at Graham Newman, and he and Graham became close friends. When Graham retired in 1956 many of his clients moved their money to Buffett's care, and they and their children and grandchildren remain Berkshire Hathaway investors today.

Just before his eightieth birthday, Graham told a friend that he hoped every day to do "something foolish, something creative, and something generous." He died at age 82 while at his second home at Aix in the south of France.

WHY DOESN'T EVERYONE DO IT?

Graham himself often pondered the mystery of why value investing concepts had been around such a long time, and had been so thoroughly proved successful, yet so few people walked the path:

> It would be rather strange if—with all the brains at work professionally in the stock market—there could be approaches which are both sound and relatively unpopular. Yet our own career and reputation have been based on this unlikely fact. [7]

Value investing as taught by Graham slips in and out of vogue over the years, invariably gaining in popularity when markets are down or uncertainty runs rampant. Investors are just as likely to suffer memory lapses when markets are rising and making money seems easy. Despite the long-term success of value investing practitioners, business schools across the nation have devoted greater attention to such concepts as the efficient market hypothesis, the capital asset pricing model, market timing, and asset allocation.

Academic journals are full of treatises purporting to prove or disprove Graham's principles and many of the other theories just mentioned. Yet as the business schools, the media, and fad investors chase one new rainbow after another, Buffett and other Graham disciples plod along, piling up profits.

SMALL PLAYERS FEEL OVERPOWERED

Even so, some investors, many laypeople in particular, shy away from the value principles because they fear that the concepts are too intellectual, that there is no room for them on the playing field, or that more sophisticated players control the game. The principles are relatively easy to grasp for those who are willing to go step by step. Though readers of this book are encouraged to learn as much as possible about stocks and their evaluation, there are fewer than a dozen core concepts to master.

Some investors feel that because there are so many mutual funds, pension funds, and institutional money managers in the market today, smaller investors get squeezed out. "Haven't the professionals spotted all the undervalued companies and snapped up all the bargain stocks?" the individual investor asks. "There's nothing left for the rest of us."

True, value investing methods are particularly useful to large-scale investors, especially those with fiduciary responsibilities. John Train, in his 1980 best-seller *The Money Masters,* claims that Graham's method "seems particularly appropriate for institutional portfolios, such as bank-managed pension funds. The method is obviously 'prudent' and systematic—bankerly, in fact."[8]

PLENTY OF PICKINGS

Yet while institutional managers sometimes work in the orchard of value investing, they do not strip the trees clean. A large mutual fund is like a giant who lumbers along, able to pick fruit only from the tree-tops. He's too big and too far away to see the lush, perfect fruit growing at the bottom of the tree, or deep down in the leaves. Individual investors, shorter and more agile, can walk right alongside the giant and find plenty to harvest.

In an article Benjamin Graham wrote in 1974, he addressed the concerns of smaller investors:

> I am convinced that an individual investor with sound principles, and soundly advised, can do distinctly better over the long pull than a large institution. Where the trust company has to confine its operation to 300 concerns or less, the individual has up to 3000 issues for his investigations and choice. Most true bargains are not available in large blocks; by this very fact, the institutions are well-nigh eliminated as competitors of the bargain hunter.[9]

POCKETS SO DEEP THAT SOME COMPANIES GET LOST

Warren Buffett's Berkshire Hathaway is an example of the difficulties faced by institutional investors. Buffett, like many managers of the giant mutual funds, can buy only substantial blocks of shares. If he didn't take large positions in big companies, he would find himself with an unmanageable jumble of small holdings, multiple positions in thousands of companies. The cost of management and the risk of simply getting out of touch with the companies he owns would be astronomical.

This does not mean that Buffett has abandoned the Graham and Dodd principles. Buffett explains it this way in his 1994 Berkshire Hathaway annual report: "The problem is not that what has worked in the past will cease to work in the future. To the contrary, we believe that our formula—the purchase at sensible prices of businesses that have good underlying economics and are run by honest and able people—is certain to produce reasonable success."

But a fat wallet, Buffett says, is the enemy of superior investment results. "And Berkshire now has a net worth of $11.9 billion compared to about $22 million when Charlie [Munger] and I began to manage the company. Though there are as many good businesses as ever, it is useless for us to make purchases that are inconsequential in relation to Berkshire's capital."

As a result, Buffett will consider buying stock in a company only if he can invest at least $100 million in it. "Given that minimum, Berkshire's investment universe has shrunk dramatically," Buffett writes. [10]

MARKET MANIPULATION

Individual investors often are put off by the suspicion that large investors, such as Buffett, actually exploit the market for their own benefit, taking advantage of what Charles Dow called "the small operator." Speculation and manipulation were particularly egregious in Dow's time, which was long before the establishment of strict stock exchange rules and of the Securities and Exchange Commission. In the current regulatory situation, manipulation, though it does crop up, is less common. And even though market manipulation was "business as usual" in his day, Dow did not believe it had a long-term influence.

"The manipulator is all-powerful for a time," Dow wrote in 1901. "He can market prices up or down. He can mislead investors, inducing them to buy when he wishes to sell, and sell when he wishes to buy; but manipulation in a stock cannot be permanent, and, in the end, the investor learns the approximate truth. His decision to keep his stock or sell it then makes a price independent of speculation and, in a large sense, indicative of true value."[11]

A PHILOSOPHY MORE THAN A FORMULA

Some critics of the value investing approach fail to be convinced that it works because they want repeated statistical, empirical, or mathematical evidence that it works. Academic studies have been conducted, in fact, that support the theory. Yet those who studied directly under Graham are careful to explain that Graham and Dodd's *Security Analysis* and Graham's *The Intelligent Investor* are not cookbooks for the investment professional. They are not laboratory handbooks. Value investing is based more on philosophy than on theorems. There is no step one, step two, and step three. Graham's purpose was to make his students use the deductive process to think for themselves.

Despite continual examination, questioning, probing, and tweaking of the Graham and Dodd concepts, the very basics—the fundamentals—remain intact.

THREE KEY CONCEPTS

When Warren Buffett talks about his training under Graham, he says that the two most important things he learned at Columbia University were

- The right attitude
- The importance of margin of safety

By listening to Buffett speak and by reading Berkshire Hathaway's annual reports, a third key Graham concept surfaces repeatedly, that of

- Intrinsic value

These are the pillars on which the value investing philosophy is built. Though each of the three concepts will be enlarged upon in future chapters, they deserve an early introduction.

THE RIGHT ATTITUDE

To be successful, a value investor must adopt the right attitude toward investing in general, and an aversion to speculation in particular. A speculation is not an investment, Graham insisted, and it is crucial to be able to distinguish between the two. What is the difference?

When it comes to speculation, we easily can be duped by glib investment experts who convince us that big words, impressive math, and lofty concepts are good reasons to let them make investment decisions on our behalf. Sometimes we even participate in our own deception. We give in to our human weakness for gambling, said Graham and Dodd:

> Even when the underlying motive of a purchase (of a security) is mere speculative greed, human nature desires to conceal this unlovely impulse behind a screen of apparent logic and good sense.[12]

There are endless ways in which investors can throw their money into the gambling ring of speculation, but the most common ploy is to "play the market." In particular, Graham frowned upon market timing. He insisted that any financial decision based solely on the prediction that the market will move up or down is a speculation.

An investment is a proposition that offers:

- Safety of capital
- A reasonable expectation of a suitable return

Knowing that your capital is safe and that you can reasonably expect a suitable return requires some investigation and analysis, though it does not require an exceptionally high IQ or math skills. Furthermore, what may appear to others to be a high-risk proposition can actually be a sound investment, if the right information is at hand. Fortunately, the information on which to base such decisions is readily available today.

MARGIN OF SAFETY

When students of investing mention the name Benjamin Graham, the next words are likely to be—"margin of safety." This isn't a difficult concept: margin of safety is that extra change a girl takes on a date in case she needs taxi fare home.

Nothing disrupts investment goals more than unexpected adversities, but calamities do happen. The information on which an investment decision was based may have been flawed; the charismatic CEO of your company may disappear while vacationing in Tahiti; or a flood could hit the distillery in which you just invested, letting brackish water into the whiskey. A margin of safety helps guard against such alarming possibilities.

Creating a safety net when investing in securities is the goal. There are various ways to do it. Graham built up his margin of safety by seeking strength in three areas:

- Evaluation of assets
- Evaluation of earning power
- Diversification

Other skilled value investors apply their own layer of insulation. For example, some achieve a margin of safety by requiring a company to have a large cache of working capital; others study cashflow and some look to patterns of dividend payment.

INTRINSIC VALUE

Value investing, as explained earlier, is a search for sound securities that sell at or below their "intrinsic value." These investments are then held until there is strong incentive to sell them. For example, the stock's price may have risen; an asset value may have declined; or a government security may no longer deliver the kind of return the investor could earn on competing securities. The most profitable path in any case is to sell the security and move the money to another investment that is intrinsically undervalued.

Graham did not invent the term *intrinsic value*, though he did endow it with greater meaning than it had before he began teaching and writing. The phrase is known to have been used in relation to the stock market as early as 1848. William Armstrong, an investment writer, described it as the principal determinant in setting the market prices of securities, though not the only factor.

Further groundwork for the intrinsic value concept was laid when Charles H. Dow was the editor and a columnist for *The Wall Street Journal.* Though Dow is most famous for his study of stock market movements, he repeatedly explained to his turn-of-the-century audience that stock prices rise and fall because of investors' perceptions of the future profitability of a company—in other words, on the stock's intrinsic value.

THE DOW HERITAGE

"It is always safe to assume that values determine prices in the long run," wrote Dow in a column on May 18, 1900. "Values have nothing to do with current fluctuations. A worthless stock can go up five points just as easily as the best, but as a result of continued fluctuations the good stock will gradually work to its investment value, while the poor one will gradually go to its value as a gambling counter or perhaps with reference to its voting power for control."[13]

In the 1940 edition of *Security Analysis*, Graham and Dodd used a now-historic company as an example of one way intrinsic value is determined:

> In 1922, prior to the boom in aviation securities, Wright Aeronautical Corporation stock was selling on the New York Stock Exchange at only $8, although it was paying a dividend of $1, had for some time been earning over $2 a share, and showed more than $8 per share in cash assets in the treasury. In this case analysis would readily have established that the intrinsic value of the issue was substantially above the market price.[14]

Graham looked at Wright Aeronautical again in 1928. By then the company was selling at $280 per share. It was paying a $2 dividend, and earning $8 per share, and the net asset value was $50 per share. Wright was still a sound company, but future prospects in no way justified its market price. The company was, by Graham's reckoning, selling substantially above its intrinsic value.

AN ARTFUL SCIENCE

In his 1994 Berkshire Hathaway annual report, Warren Buffett spent several pages explaining how he arrives at intrinsic value. Buffett regularly reports per share book value for Berkshire Hathaway, as most investors expect. "Just as regularly we tell you that what counts is intrinsic value, a number that is impossible to pinpoint but essential to estimate."[15] However, he continues, "we define intrinsic value as the discounted value of the cash that can be taken out of a business during the remaining life." Though Buffett says this is a subjective number that changes as estimates of future cashflow are revised and as interest rates change, it still has enormous meaning.

Buffett used his 1986 purchase of the conglomerate Scott Fetzer Inc. to illustrate the point. When it was acquired by Berkshire Hathaway, Scott Fetzer had $172.6 million in book value. Berkshire paid $315.2 million for the company, a premium of $142.6 million. Between 1986 and 1994, Scott Fetzer had total earnings of $55.4 million and paid $634 million in dividends to Berkshire. Dividends were higher than earnings because the company held excess cash, or retained earnings, which it turned over to its owner—Berkshire.

As a result, Berkshire (of which Buffett himself owns more than 60 percent) tripled its investment in 3 years. Berkshire still owned Scott Fetzer, which had virtually the same book value that it did when Buffett bought it. Yet since purchasing the company, Berkshire has earned double the acquisition price in dividends.

Some analysts consider net current asset value to be a measure of intrinsic value. Others focus on price-earnings ratio or other, more fluid factors. Whatever device investors may use, the goal is to find an estimate of a company's present and future worth.

"Almost by definition, a really good business generates far more money (at least after its early years) than it can use internally," explains Buffett. That money can be reinvested to increase the value of the company or paid out to shareholders in dividends. One way or another, this additional money will eventually work its way back to the shareholders.[16]

CONCLUSION

Value investing principles can apply to all classes of securities, including preferred stocks, municipal bonds, corporate bonds, and mutual funds. Each of these types of securities has evolved considerably since *Security Analysis* and *The Intelligent Investor* were last revised, but the basic tenets still apply. Nevertheless, so that the scope of *Value Investing Made Easy* will be manageable within the pages allotted, most of our attention will be focused on common stocks.

In the chapters ahead we will further study both margin of safety and intrinsic value by learning to identify safety in the balance sheet and growth prospects in the income statement. One of Graham's methods of selecting stock, the net asset value method, leans heavily on balance sheet information. The second, earnings power, relies on the income statement.

Later in the book we will explore ways to rate management, select an individual stock, structure a portfolio, manage risk, and take advantage of special investment opportunities. Value investors never try to anticipate movements on the stock market, but Graham's principles can help investors protect themselves when euphoria hits Wall Street or take advantage of the Street's shortsightedness when gloom descends.

IN THE MEANTIME, REMEMBER

- Value investing has allowed many investors to maintain consistent returns of 17 percent a year and higher, defying the contention that nobody can beat the market today because all investors have access to the same information at the same time—and that markets are therefore efficient. "I'd be a bum on the street with a tin cup if the markets were efficient," says Buffett.[17]

- Unlike a speculation, an investment offers safety of capital plus a reasonable expectation of an appropriate return.

- Don't gamble on market swings. With securities, value determines price in the long run.

- Margin of safety is the extra strength engineers build into bridges, airplanes, and high-rise buildings in the event their worst-case scenario wasn't imaginative enough.

- Peter Lynch, former manager of Fidelity Magellan Fund, says the question of what makes a company more valuable tomorrow than it is today always comes down to two things—earnings and assets. Though sometimes it takes years for a company's share price to catch up to its value, it invariably happens. "Value always wins out —or at least in enough cases that it's worthwhile to believe it," Lynch writes.[18]

2 Safety in the Balance Sheet

Diamonds are a girl's best friend.

SONGWRITER LEO ROBIN

Investors also like assets to be tangible, enduring, and to glitter.

E arly in his career, Graham invested skillfully by ferreting out information on a company's assets and interpreting their value to investors. Though the focus of his search for the intrinsic value of a company's shares later shifted to earnings, Graham continued to believe that assets, as revealed on the balance sheet, were fundamental to understanding stocks and to building a solid portfolio that would deliver high returns over an extended period of time:

> On numerous occasions prior to this point we have expressed our conviction that the balance sheet deserves more attention than Wall Street has been willing to accord it for many years past.[1]

To novice investors, it is often bothersome to study financial statements at all, and to the uninitiated, they are unintelligible. Even to a more experienced investor, the rows and rows of numbers can be intimidating. Fortunately, only a few key figures and ratios are essential to investment decisions. Graham taught the importance of numbers because he knew that "what you see is what you get." Graham understood WYSIWYG long before computer programmers invented the acronym.

WYSIWYG INVESTING

In general terms (intrinsic value) is understood to be that value which is justified by the facts, e.g., the assets, earnings, dividends, definite prospects, as distinct, let us say, from market quotations established by artificial manipulation or distorted by psychological excesses.[2]

While some securities analysts believe that only a limited number of these "facts" can be found in the balance sheet, others disagree. These counterconvictions often create competing camps, even among value investors.

HOW TRUSTWORTHY ARE THE NUMBERS?

Benjamin Graham was an unrelenting critic of "creative accounting," and sometimes wrote satirical pieces on the subject. In one he lampooned U.S. Steel, a favorite target, for creating value in its "experimental accounting laboratory." With Securities and Exchange Commission surveillance and the vigilance of the Financial Accounting Standards Board (FASB), few accountants and chief financial officers would put their careers at risk by falsifying the numbers. It would be naive to believe, however, that companies no longer put a spin on the numbers.

"Deliberate falsification of the data is rare; most of the misrepresentation flows from the use of accounting artifices, which it is the function of the capable analyst to detect. Concealment is more common than misstatement."[3]

The misrepresentations can be so subtle that even professional investors are puzzled by them. For example, in 1994 the FASB tried to require that the value of stock options and other issuances be recorded as compensation expense on a company's income statement. Corporate officers, the primary recipients of options, lobbied vigorously and even rallied Congress to pressure the FASB and the Securities and Exchange

Commission to maintain the status quo.

"One could argue that if stock options have no value," said Frank K. Martin, an investment manager from Indiana, "why are they issued in the first place? And if they do have worth, as a glance at the options page in *The Wall Street Journal* plainly confirms, what are they if not an expense? The fact that they cannot be valued precisely makes them no less an expense than depreciation, which itself only approximates the wearing out of an asset."[4]

When "deliberate falsifications" occur, there are warning signals that something is amiss. Among the red flares are qualifying remarks in the auditor's statement, constant disagreements between corporate officials and their auditors, frequent changes of auditors, or repeated switches from one form of depreciation to another.

There are no analyst's adjustments, or discounting of this item or that, that can compensate for accounting shenanigins. When an investor finds that management is playing tricks with the accounting statement, the investor should simply move on in search of another company. Trust is essential where securities are concerned.

"When an enterprise pursues questionable accounting policies, all of its securities must be shunned by the investor, no matter how safe or attractive some of them may appear."[5]

THE GREAT DEBATE

Walter Schloss and Irving Kahn, seasoned investors who both worked and studied with Graham, still emphasize the balance sheet. Buffett places greater weight on the income statement. All three make money.

Schloss, who joined the Graham Newman Co. when he returned from serving in World War II and went out on his own in 1955, has been beating the Standard & Poor's 500 since before there was an S&P 500. For 39 years he has earned an average annual return of slightly more than 20 percent. And he's done it while using a low-risk strategy. Schloss trusts balance sheets because he says they are less easily manipulated than are income statements.[6]

Kahn, who for decades served as Graham's teaching assistant at Columbia and who, at age 90, still runs a remarkably successful New York investment firm, bases his attitude on tradition. "We stress balance sheets and assets. We're old-fashioned because our paramount aim is preservation of capital. We want to buy only those securities where there's a reasonable chance of preserving your capital," Kahn says.

His son Thomas, a partner in the family firm, explains further. "Stocks rarely get priced at sharp discounts from intrinsic value without the market perceiving, correctly or incorrectly, that there are troubles in the company. Our job is to analyze whether those troubles are permanent or temporary."[7]

Buffett notes, however, that focus on the balance sheet is more effective when working with smaller pools of money. He particularly abandoned Graham's preference for tangible assets over intangibles. When cranking higher returns from enormous sums of money, intangibles give earnings a lift.

A BALANCED POINT OF VIEW

There is a legitimacy to the balance sheet versus income statement debate, which Graham himself recognized. Few investors can deny that income is an important element in choosing stocks wisely. Graham and Dodd pointed out, that the value of a common stock depends entirely on future earnings. On the other hand, Graham said, there are no guarantees:

> Observation over many years has taught us that the chief losses to investors come from the purchase of low-quality securities at times of favorable business conditions. The purchasers view the current good earnings as equivalent to "earnings power" and assume that prosperity is synonymous with safety.[8]

KISSING COUSIN TO THE INCOME STATEMENT

The truth is that to get a full picture of a company, we must look at both the balance sheet and income statement. By doing so, we can make "a twofold test of value," one test from balance sheet information and a second test from the income statement.[9]

There are three main elements to study when evaluating a company for investment potential. The first two are found on the balance sheet; the third on the income statement:

- Worth and quality of assets say much about a company's stability, safety, and in special cases, potential increase in share price.
- Debt cuts into assets and earnings, but also can stimulate corporate growth.
- Earnings quality and potential form the primary basis of share price growth.

Precisely because there is so much emphasis today on earnings power we, being contrarians by nature, will start with the balance sheet. The balance sheet can be dry ground for sure. The following discussion will try to make it fascinating, but failing that, I pledge to make it simple by prospecting the balance sheet like an investor, not like an accountant. What we are looking for on those gray pages are signs of that all-important but elusive concept—a dollar amount that we can call the intrinsic value of a stock.

COMFORT AND SWEET SURPRISES

The first rule of business for a value investor is to not lose money, and this is where the balance sheet becomes worth whatever basic training is required. Balance sheet news can be negative, positive, or neutral. It can tell you if a company is likely to go broke or to stagnate, or whether it is bedrock solid. The numbers found on a balance sheet can also suggest the lower limits of intrinsic value—the price below which the share price becomes a true bargain.

A balance sheet can send warning signs, but it also can offer comforting reassurance regarding the safety of an investment. When intrinsic value is confirmed in the balance sheet, the investor can feel confident that the company will be around and churning out returns for a long time.

The balance sheet also can reveal unusual rewards for the investor, Graham noted:

> When the cash holdings are exceptionally large in relation to the market price of the securities, this factor usually

deserves a favorable investment attention. In such cases, the stock may be worth more than the earning record indicates, because a good part of the value is represented by cash holdings which contribute little to the income account. Eventually the stockholders are likely to get the benefit of these cash assets, either through their distribution or their more productive use in the business.[10]

More about cash holdings later in this chapter when we talk about asset plays.

WHAT IS A BALANCE SHEET?

A balance sheet is sometimes called a statement of condition, and that's a good description. It is a financial "snapshot," clicked at a specific moment in a corporation's life—say, the end of an operating period such as a quarter or a fiscal year. "One way of looking at a business enterprise is as a mass of capital (assets) arrayed against the sources of that capital (liabilities and equity)," explain John Downes and Jordan Goodman in their *Dictionary of Finance and Investment Terms.* "Assets are equal to liabilities and equity and the balance sheet is a listing of the items making up the two sides of the equation."[11]

The financial statements are full of quantitative measures.

- Quantitative factors are those bits of investment information that lend themselves to mathematical analysis. Fortunately, those quantitative factors can be reduced to a few simple guidelines that anyone can understand.

Ultimately, the balance sheet quantitative factors are only a way to screen stocks for the next step, qualitative analysis.

- Qualitative factors are those that lend themselves to intellectualization—they require us to use our reasoning power. Qualitative factors include the nature of the business, the relative position of the company in the industry, its physical, geographic, and operating characteristics, its management, and finally its outlook for the industry and the economy in general.

In the end, the balance sheet and income statement tell about the things that make a stock worth buying. A pocket calculator can help interpret the numbers, but only an investor can decide whether to buy a stock.

WHAT A BALANCE SHEET TELLS YOU

The key balance sheet indicators are

- Assets
- Debt
- Cash position
- Equity position (plus dividends)

These figures, however, have little meaning unless they are considered in relationship to one another. Often the numbers are compared by ratios, or they are divided by the number of common shares outstanding and compared with the company's share price. Comparing a company's ratios with those of its competitors or its industry in general puts the numbers in perspective.

READING FINANCIAL STATEMENTS

The debt-to-equity ratio, working capital, current ratio, and quick ratio (acid test) all derive from the balance sheet. Ultraconservative investors also compare a company's book value with its share price to see if the stock is a bargain. Others claim that book value means nothing. More about that quarrel later.

It all begins, nevertheless, with a look at assets.

When looking at any financial statement numbers, do a comparison over time. Most corporate annual reports present figures for the current year compared with the previous year, and some companies include charts showing changes over multiple years. Analytical services, such as Value Line and Standard & Poor's, offer historic information up to 10 years. The numbers of a single year reveal little about the stability and growth of the business. Year-to-year comparisons of both the balance sheet and income statement show a progression of events. Any company can have its ups and downs, but if share price is to increase, the company must, over a period of time, grow.

AN INVESTOR'S VIEW OF ASSETS

For an investor, asset value is like a safety net. A share price may fall, but it is highly unlikely to fall through the net. That net also can give bounce to a share price. If a stock is undervalued in terms of its assets, something will happen so that the asset value of the stock will be fully actualized. That "something" may be a natural rise in the share price, a takeover bid, or most unusual of all, a liquidation of assets and payment of cash to shareholders in the form of a special dividend.

While liquidation seldom takes place, it came close to happening not long ago to a very large company. General Dynamics, its share price staggering from news that the cold war had ended and U.S. military spending would be slashed, immediately enacted an aggressive plan to turn part of its $3.9 billion assets into cash and to preserve the wealth of some major shareholders.

ASSETS CAN BE RECYCLED

The 100-year-old military contractor sold its tactical military operations, space systems, Cessna division, and data processing operation. These sales reduced GD's business to nuclear submarines and armored military vehicles (tanks), two areas in which management believed GD could be market leaders. In 1992, while the restructuring was in progress, Buffett bought 15 percent of the company.

At the same time the company conducted an unusual type of stock sale called a "Dutch auction" to allow GD's largest shareholders, the Crown family of Chicago, to cash in some of their investment. In 1993, GD bought back about 30 percent of its stock and that year paid a total of $50 per share in special cash distribution (in addition to regular dividends) to shareholders, the Crowns included. The special distribution amounted to $50 per share.

When all the work was done, GD's long-term debt was cut to practically nothing; its sales were slashed by nearly one-third; but its total market capital (the price for which you could buy all the company's shares) rose from $1 billion in 1991 to $3 billion in 1995. GD's share price shot from a low of $9.5 in 1990 to a high of $60 in 1993. After GD fervor cooled, the share price fell for a while, but was trading back at $59 in early 1996.

In 1995, GD still held $1.2 billion in cash (nearly $18 per share), which ordinarily might make it a target for a hostile leveraged buyout. However, since the Crown family still owned 13 percent of the shares and Berkshire Hathaway owned 8.4 percent (following the cash distribution, Berkshire sold some shares), any takeover offer would have to be a persuasive one.

ASSET PLAYS

During the period of downsizing, General Dynamics was an asset play. "An asset play is any company that's sitting on something valuable that you know about, but that the Wall Street crowd has overlooked," explains Peter Lynch.[12]

Lynch points out that the old, publicly traded railroads such as Burlington Northern, Union Pacific, and Santa Fe Southern Pacific are real estate rich, dating back to the government land giveaway of the nineteenth century to encourage railroad construction. Not only did the railroads get land, they got the oil, gas, mineral, and timber rights as well. By the end of the twentieth century, the nature of transportation had changed and railroads were capitalizing less on their rolling stock and more on their natural resource assets. Assets made the railroads valuable.

NOT ALL ASSETS ARE EQUAL

The demarcation between old-time value investors—those who keep a wary eye out for a repeat of the Crash of 1929—and the new-era investors such as Buffett is their attitude regarding certain types of assets. The conservative investors place their faith in tangible assets. The more contemporary thinkers say they get greater momentum on total return by demanding fewer tangible assets and by understanding intangibles better.

Warren Buffett says that he achieved some of his greatest successes when he kicked the tangible asset habit. "Keynes [John Maynard] identified my problem. 'The difficulty lies not in the new ideas but in escaping from the old ones.' My escape was long delayed, in part because most of what I had been taught by the same teacher had been (and continues to be) so extraordinarily valuable. Ultimately, business experience, directed and vicarious, produced my present strong preference for businesses that possess large amounts of enduring goodwill and that utilize a minimum of tangible assets."[13] Coca Cola and Geico are good examples of such Berkshire Hathaway holdings.

HARD ASSETS

Tangibles include both cash and fixed assets such as land, buildings, equipment, and office furnishings. Fixed assets, especially if they are paid for and have appreciated and are carried at less than their actual current value, can be important. Old companies like the railroads, AT&T, Du Pont, and many public utilities, have seen their share price appreciate because of the growing value of some of their fixed assets.

Yet even the value of tangible assets can be questionable. Tangibles should be measured on a sliding scale. Cash assets can be accepted at face value, whereas buildings, machinery, nonmarketable investments, and so forth may be worth up to half (or less) of their stated value. Real estate is tricky, since its sale price is negotiable and depends on many different factors.

SOFT ASSETS

The of value of intangibles is even more elusive. Intangibles include goodwill, patents and trademarks, licenses, capitalized advertising costs, and other nonphysical resources that give a company some foothold or advantage in the marketplace. Coca Cola's world-famous logo is one example. It is nearly impossible to put a price on these assets, though companies make logical, and sometimes very sophisticated, estimates.

Graham and Dodd were not known for their love of intangibles, but they knew that earnings on intangibles are less vulnerable to competition than assets that require only a cash investment:

Under modern conditions the so-called "intangibles," goodwill or even a highly efficient organization, are every whit as real from a dollars and cents standpoint as are buildings and machinery. Furthermore, when conditions are favorable the enterprise with the relatively small capital investment is likely to show a more rapid rate of growth. Ordinarily it can expand its sales and profits at slight expense and therefore grow more rapidly and profitably for its stockholders than a business requiring a large plant investment per dollar of sales.[14]

LIQUIDATING VALUE OF ASSETS

	Percent of Liquidating Value to Book Value	
TYPE OF ASSET	NORMAL RANGE	ROUGH AVERAGE
Current assets: cash assets (including securities at market)	100	100
Current assets: receivables (less usual reserves)*	75–90	80
Current assets: inventories (at lower of cost or market)	50–75	66 2/3
Fixed and miscellaneous assets: real estate, buildings, machinery, equipment, nonmarketable investments, intangibles	1–50	15 (approx.)

*Retail installment accounts must be valued for liquidation at a lower rate. The range is about 30–60%; the average, about 50%.

Source: *Security Analysis* (New York: McGraw-Hill, 1940), p. 579.

BOOK VALUE, BUT DOES ANYONE CARE?

If the debate over tangibles versus intangibles gets scrappy, there is less argument about book value. Many serious investors pay little heed to it. This may confuse readers of annual reports, stock analyses, and other publications which faithfully relate book value.

Book value once was considered the most important element in a corporate financial report, but that was the olden days. Things changed when investors realized that asset values often show no relationship to their original cost, the price at which they could be sold, or even their future replacement cost. Accountants struggle to make the books reflect actual value, a goal that is virtually impossible to achieve. Nobody knows how much most assets (other than cash and equivalents) will fetch in the marketplace until they are sold.

When asked about the importance of book value at his 1995 Berkshire Hathaway annual meeting, Buffet said, "Book value is not a consideration. What we consider more important is the generation of high returns on capital employed."[15] Book value, he noted, is rooted in the past. It is the historical input, while intrinsic value is the future output. The problem is that many analysts confuse book value with intrinsic value. To repeat a point made earlier, book value (when it is stated with reasonable accuracy) is the price below which intrinsic value can never fall. And if all goes well, the company will be worth much more than book value.

What is this oft-quoted number of questionable importance?

$$\text{Book value} = \frac{\text{total assets} - \text{intangible assets} - \text{liabilities} - \text{stock issues ahead of the common stock}}{\text{number of common shares}}$$

The Wall Street Journal once gave this example of how Graham used book value: "A company with $2 billion in assets and $1.6 billion in liabilities has a book value of $400 million. If it has 20 million shares of common stock outstanding, its per share book value is $20. So Graham wouldn't pay more than $24 for the stock."[16]

A typical company on the stock market today trades at about three times its book value. Graham said that desirable stocks should sell for less than 1.2 times tangible book value per share, and less is better.

WE CARE:
BOOK VALUE ISN'T DEAD YET

Despite its admitted weaknesses, book value is a useful measure of what is being paid for the actual assets of the company. For those following

Graham's admonition to buy a stock as if you were buying a business, book value is an informative number. It tells a buyer what she is getting for her money. If it were possible to achieve the same or better return on investment by buying a similar asset at a lower price and starting a new company, it might be smart to do so. In fact, said Graham and Dodd, that is exactly what creates competition for successful companies:

> There are indeed certain presumptions in favor of purchases made far below asset value and against those made at a high premium above it. A business that sells at a premium does so because it earns a large return on its capital; this large return attracts competition, and, generally speaking, it is not likely to continue indefinitely.[17]

The reverse is generally true of a company selling at a discount to asset value because of abnormally low earnings, they said:

> We do not think, therefore, that any rules may reasonably be laid down on the subject of book value in relation to market price, except the strong recommendation already made that the purchaser know what he is doing on this score and be satisfied in his own mind that he is acting sensibly.[18]

It was no coincidence that Chase Manhattan Bank was trading below book value in 1995 when investor Michael F. Price took a 6.1 percent share in the company and began pressuring management to "maximize value." Price wanted management to do something to get the share price up. Soon afterward Chase launched aggressive cost-cutting measures at the bank and in August 1995 announced it would merge with Chemical Bank in a $10 billion stock swap. The merger, investors hope, will result in an increase in return on assets.

THE DEBT QUESTIONS

Once an investor has contemplated the nature of corporate assets, there are two additional questions to ask of a balance sheet:

- Is debt manageable?
- Once debts are taken care of, is there enough cash left to perpetuate the business?

Most of us understand debt at a gut level. It's a lesson we've learned from our personal lives. Debt is both healthy and hazardous. Prudent loans for education, houses, cars, and other major assets can improve our financial position. Short-term borrowing smooths budgeting bumps. Excessive borrowing can put us in the poorhouse. It is the same for corporations.

As Peter Lynch reminds us: "Companies that have no debt can't go bankrupt."[19]

On the positive side, debt obligation adds to the funds available to the corporation. Graham and Dodd pointed out that debt is part of capital structure and as such gives the company a greater ability to finance new construction, develop new products, or expand into additional markets:

> The optimum capitalization structure for any enterprise includes senior securities to the extent that they may safely be issued and bought for investment.[20]

Buffett concurs. "We're far from believing that there is not a fate worse than debt. We are willing to borrow an amount that we believe—on a worst-case basis—will pose no threat to Berkshire's well-being," he wrote.[21]

LET THE RATIOS BEGIN

Yet because large bank debt is a common sign of financial weakness, analysts routinely apply several tests to gauge a company's debtworthiness. The first measure is the debt-to-equity ratio, which indicates the ownership standing behind borrowed money. It shows the extent to which equity can cushion creditors' claims in the event of liquidation.

$$\text{Debt-to-equity ratio} = \frac{\text{total liabilities}}{\text{shareholder equity}}$$

Ordinarily, a company should have an approximate debt-to-equity ratio of 50 percent. In other words, investors want $1 of equity for every 50 cents (or when everything else is sound, stretched to 55 cents) of debt. For more conservative investors, debt should be no more than 50 percent of total capital, and never should debt exceed 55 percent of total capital.

A second way an investor can evaluate a company's debt position is by checking the rating on its corporate bonds, which in turn impacts the interest rate that corporations pay on borrowed money, advise Graham and Dodd:

> A common stock representing the entire business cannot be less safe than a bond having a claim for only a part thereof.[22]

IT'S EASY TO BORROW WHEN YOU DON'T NEED TO

Financial writer James Grant refers to the bond-rating check as Graham and Dodd's first law of credit. "Allowance must be made for the fact that the rate of interest tends to vary inversely with the ability of the company to pay it. A strong company borrows at a low rate, although it could afford to pay more than could a weak company. This means that 'good credit' itself produces 'better credit' through its own saving of interest charges, whereas the opposite is equally true. Although this may seem paradoxical and unfair, it must be accepted as a fact in security analysis."[23]

Bonds are rated by several credit rating companies. The major ones are Standard & Poor's, Moody's Investors Service, and Fitch's Investor Service. Their ratings range from AAA (highly unlikely to default) to D (in danger of default). Investment-grade bonds are rated BB and above. S&P also rates stocks in its analytical reports, and this can be a useful measure of quality.

NET CURRENT ASSET VALUE

Working capital is an especially useful financial cushion. Net current asset value, or working capital, is the money a company uses to finance its daily operations, or business cycle. That cycle begins with raw materials, progresses to finished goods and sales, and finally results in cash register receipts.

Net current asset value (working capital) = current assets (cash, accounts receivable, inventory) – current liabilities

By pairing stability and management with an analysis of working capital, an investor gets an idea of management's ability not only to cope with changing economic conditions but to maintain growth. Working capital shows that a company has the resources to pay its current obligations from its current assets.

Net current asset value is at the base of Graham's investment theories. Whenever possible, investors want to purchase stocks at two-thirds the net current asset value per share. Such stocks can be difficult to find, and when they are found, they must be studied to learn why they are selling for so cheap a price. The current ratio is another standard way of measuring working capital.

$$\text{Current ratio} = \frac{\text{current assets}}{\text{current liabilities}}$$

A similar standard is used for the current ratio as is used for debt-to-equity ratio. A sound company should have a current ratio of 2—that is, no more than $1 of current liability for $2 of current assets. Stated another way, a current ratio of 2 indicates a debt of no more than 50 percent of current assets. Generally, a company with a small inventory and easily collectible accounts receivable can operate safely with a lower current ratio than a company whose cashflow is less dependable.

THE ACID TEST

An even more rigorous measure of the everyday working strength of a company is its quick ratio, which is also called the acid test. It is based on net quick assets.

Net quick asset value = current assets – inventory – current liabilities

$$\text{Quick ratio (acid test)} = \frac{\text{current assets} - \text{inventory}}{\text{current liabilities}}$$

A quick ratio of 1 shows the ability to meet obligations in the event that all sales would stop. An investor can ask that a company pass both the current ratio and the quick ratio tests.

LIQUIDATING VALUE

When looking at the current asset value, we're getting down to a notion that few investors care to ponder—the liquidating value. Following the Great Depression the share price of public companies fell so low that many investors bought in just to sell off the companies' assets and close their operations. Liquidating a company is not a pleasant prospect, since workers lose their jobs, communities lose their income base, and society in general suffers. The liquidating value is not only the end of the line; it can be seen as the absolute bottom line. There is no question that the ultimate intrinsic value is revealed when liquidation occurs.

The net current asset value (working capital) per share described earlier also is a rough index of liquidating value. The liquidating value of a company is never a hard number. It can only be estimated, until a company actually is sold off. This is attributed to a fact we noted earlier. It sometimes is called Graham and Dodd's first rule of liquidating value:

> The liabilities are real but the value of the assets must be questioned.[24]

Fortunately, advise Graham and Dodd, it is enough to get a rough idea of the liquidating value for most purposes, accepting the fact that you won't get, nor will you actually need, an exact figure.

A share price below liquidating value seldom is good news. Temporary conditions—a big stock market drop, a sudden reaction to shocking bad news—may impact a company to that extent. Very quickly, however, the share price should recover. When a stock persistently sells below its liquidating value, it indicates an error in judgment by someone—management, shareholders, or the stock market in general.

WAKE UP, MANAGEMENT

> There can be no sound economic reason for a stock's selling continuously below its liquidation value. If the company is

not worth more as a going concern than in liquidation, it should be liquidated.[25]

If management doesn't resolve the problem, Graham and Dodd continue, investors should:

> The fact that an issue sells below liquidating value is a signal that mistaken policies are being followed and that therefore the management should take corrective action—if not voluntarily, then under pressure from the stockholders.[26]

As depression era investors realized, even a company selling below liquidating value can make a good investment if circumstances are advantageous. Industry conditions may be rising dramatically. There may be improvements in the company's operating policy, such as a change in management, new products, or abandonment of an archaic product. The company may be seen as a takeover target. Or the assets may indeed be liquidated and the money distributed to shareholders.

The risk in buying a stock selling under liquidating value—and it is a substantial risk—is that the company will continue to lose money and that the owners will not liquidate. In fact, owners and managers seldom liquidate until bankruptcy proceedings force them do so.

NET NETS

Investors can't go far wrong by buying a well-diversified basket of companies whose current assets are one-third greater than the sum of current *and* long-term liabilities. This is the "used cigar butt" approach Warren Buffett described in Chapter 1. These so-called net net stocks are difficult to find today, but occasionally they do surface. If there is a bare-bones Graham technique, this is it. This is how he shopped at a Wall Street fire sale. Following the Great Depression, Graham made a fortune buying net net stocks. He paid little attention to quality, but bought a large number of them, seeking protection through diversification.

$$\text{Net net asset value per share} = \frac{\text{current assets} - \text{current liabilities} - \text{long-term debt}}{\text{number of shares outstanding}}$$

A stock selling at one-third below the net net asset value can be considered a steal, even if its financial condition is somewhat battered.

OWNERSHIP INFORMATION

Owner's equity, as mentioned earlier, is a combination of preferred and common stock, retained earnings, and a few other items. As a shareholder, your name is engraved here. It is your ambition, as an owner, to see, one way or another, a return on your investment. The return can be an increase in share price, a payment of dividends, or both. How much is considered a suitable return on equity will be addressed in the next chapter.

PAR VALUE

At one time par value meant the amount of money invested in the business. It was the original price paid for each share of stock, and therefore was a measure of the shareholder's initial investment. It was a yardstick of growth over the life of a business. Corporations now assign arbitrary par values to shares for accounting purposes only. Shareholder equity takes on a meaning similar to the old par value, though it isn't always easy to learn what the original shareholder equity was. Once an informative number, par value for a stock, though it is still reported in accounting statements has entirely lost its meaning to investors.

THOSE DIVINE DIVIDENDS

Dividends represent nothing more than the investor's share of earnings that will be received immediately (rather than through reinvestment and future growth of the stock). Dividends are one of the quickest and healthiest ways that earnings can make their way into shareholders' pockets.

One of the most controversial concepts of Graham and Dodd is that it is not necessarily in the best interest of shareholders for management to withhold earnings rather than pay dividends:

> Although investors have been taught to pay lip service to this theory (that plowing profits back into the business is always best), their instincts—and perhaps their better judgment—are in revolt against it.[27]

Graham argued that intelligent investors would rather have dividends in their pockets (even if investors use them to buy more of the same stock) than risk waiting for possible future growth. Furthermore, he insisted, it is management's responsibility to pay dividends:

> I believe that Wall Street experience shows clearly that the best treatment for stockholders is the payment to them of fair and reasonable dividends in relation to the company's earnings and in relation to the true value of the security, as measured by any ordinary tests based on earnings power or assets.[28]

Graham contended that when corporate management is stingy with dividends or withholds them altogether, it's sometimes for self-serving reasons. It's easier to keep the cash on hand to bail management out of bad times or bad decisions. Sometimes the dividend policy is simply a reflection of the tax status of management and large investors—they don't want the addition to their current taxable income. Consequently, other investors get no income.

MORE THAN AN OLD FOLKS' REWARD

While attention to dividends is not as voguish as it once was, especially with money managers who are looking for the fast spurts of share price growth, individual investors or safety seekers may want them. For long-term investors who follow a "buy and hold" strategy, dividends are the only way to collect on investment gains.

In addition to representing money in the bank, dividends are, to many investors, a reliable indicator of future growth. The awareness of a relationship between dividends and intrinsic value goes way back. "Values are determined roughly by the earnings available for dividends," wrote Charles Dow in 1902. At that time the major stock investments were railroads, and the major motivation was to earn dividends. However, the relation among earnings, dividends, and values survives.[29]

A long history of dividend payments and regular dividend increases also indicates a substantial company with limited risk. Additionally, a rise in the dividend is tangible confirmation of the confidence of management in good times ahead. A cut in the dividend is a red flag indicating trouble on the track.

Not all corporate income need be paid in dividends. Depending on the industry and how much capital is required to keep the business growing, the appropriate payout may be as much as 80 percent or as little as 50 percent of net earnings. When studying the dividend payout of a company, calculate both average earnings and average dividends over a 10-year period. From those two averages you can determine the average payout. Earnings fluctuate, but dividends tend to remain stable or, in the best companies, to rise gradually.

TOTAL RETURN

There undoubtedly is some trade-off between dividends and share price appreciation, and that is why total return—dividends plus share price growth—is the yardstick by which all investments are measured. The WD-40 Co., maker of the spray lubricant, is typical of a stock with an honorable dividend history and a high payout.

WD-40 DIVIDENDS

Year	1986	1987	1988	1989	1990	1991	1992	1993	1994	1995
Dividend	1.04	1.47	1.63	1.90	2.02	1.72	2.16	2.30	2.30	2.50
Dividend as a percent of net income	67	100	79	91	99	85	91	85	86	89

Source: 1995 WD-40 annual report.

During the late 1980s WD-40 saturated the U.S. market with its sole product, and the company was forced to seek expansion internationally. Not only was the effort costly, but sales flattened during the time new markets were being developed. The dividend history tells the story. Net income varied from year to year, but except for 1991, the dividend rose. The result was a higher percentage of payout in some years than in others. The dividend record shows that management had faith in the company's growth strategy. In 1995 WD-40's dividend yield was 5.9 percent, and the stock was considered by most analysts to be a value buy.

One way of determining if a stock is overvalued or undervalued is to compare its dividend yield with that of similar companies. Safety, growth, and other factors being equal, the stock with the highest dividend and the lowest share price is the best bargain. As a further check of value, investors should compare the stock's dividend yield with that of the Dow Jones Industrial Average. That figure is frequently reported in *The Wall Street Journal,* and *Barron's* and by such analytical services as Value Line and Standard & Poor's.

GETTING YOUR EQUITY IN SMALLER BITS?

Graham differed from other analysts in his attitude toward stock dividends. Management and analysts alike often see stock dividends as merely reducing the value of those shares already outstanding. Graham observed, however, that a stock dividend could be used as a way to transfer accumulated reserves into the capital structure of the company. If the dividend is nondilutive and if it really is a distribution of accumulated capital, the share price may suffer initially but will ultimately rise. In time, investors will benefit.

There also is generally a negative attitude among investors toward stock splits. Usually the goal of a split is to reduce the share price and make the stock more liquid. After a split the investor has more shares, but each share will be worth less. If a company pays a regular dividend, however, shareholders reap the benefit of multiplied dividend payments. The split shares usually pay the same dividend as did shares prior to the split. Automatically the dollar amount of dividends received is increased by the increment of the split (doubled, tripled, and so on). Though the share price may go down, the investor's total return (dividend plus share price increase) may suffer very little. If the split was done for the right reasons, the share price often begins to rise again soon after the split. In cases where no dividend is involved, the objection to a stock split or stock dividend is valid. It truly does not give shareholders anything they didn't own before.

RATIONALE FOR WITHHOLDING DIVIDENDS

Certainly some reliable, fast-growing companies do not pay dividends. Buffett hasn't paid a cash dividend since 1967, when he still operated a limited partnership. Yet that partnership and its successor, Berkshire Hathaway, have transformed many dozens of ordinary investors into millionaires. On the other hand, investors must sell shares if they need cash, and with each Berkshire Hathaway share trading at close to $36,000 (as of March, 1996) selling shares can be a real inconvenience.

If a company isn't paying dividends it should, like Berkshire Hathaway, be doing something profitable with its earnings. It is acceptable to withhold dividends for the following reasons:

• To strengthen the company's working capital
• To increase productive capacity
• To reduce debt

DIVIDENDS IN JEOPARDY

Dividends may be put in jeopardy in two ways:

• When a company's earnings per share is less than its dividend per share
• When debt is excessive

A company's average earnings (over several years) should be sufficient to cover its average dividend. Though earnings per share can fall below dividend per share from time to time with reserves making up the difference, the condition can persist for only so long.

A company with substantial earnings rarely becomes insolvent because of bank loans. But when a company is under pressure, lenders may require a suspension of dividends as a form of financial discipline.

CONCLUSION

Home buyers are cautioned to look for a house built on solid ground, above a flood plain, and with a strong foundation. Investors should heed similar advice. A good balance sheet is a firm foundation for any company. And for both a house and an investment, a smart buyer doesn't pay more than an asset is worth.

Graham and Dodd remind us that on its own, a price close to asset value doesn't guarantee a hefty total return down the line. But it is a first step in identifying a value investment. A good price-to-earnings ratio, low costs, good products, strong sales, and good future earnings prospects tell the rest of the story.

IN THE MEANTIME, REMEMBER

- The balance sheet is a valuable tool. Don't be intimidated by it.
- Safety, in regard to investing, is never absolute and complete. However, we can significantly improve our chances of success by boldly going where few dare to go—to the financial statements.
- Though not the intrinsic value—or the future value to an owner— book value can be seen as a floor on intrinsic value.
- Think of the corporation as a ship. The balance sheet is the hull; the income statement is the sails. The hull keeps it afloat but the sails (sales?) make the boat move.

FORMULAS AND RATIOS AT A GLANCE

- Book Value $= \frac{TA - IC - AL - SI}{S}$

- Debt/Equity $= \frac{AL}{SE}$

- Net Current Asset Value $= CA - CL$

- Current Ratio $= \frac{CA}{CL}$

- Net Quick Asset Value $= CA - I - CL$

- Quick Ratio $= \frac{CA - I}{CL}$

- Net Net $= CA - CL - LTD$

- Net Net Current Assets per Share $= \frac{CA - CL - LTD}{S}$

- Price/Earnings Ratio $= \frac{SP}{E}$

- Profit Margin $= \frac{GP}{TS}$

TA = Total Assets
IC = Intangible Assets
AL = All Liabilities
SI = Stock Issues
S = Number of Common Shares Outstanding
SE = Total Shareholders Equity
CA = Current Assets
CL = Current Liabilities
I = Inventory
LTD = Long-Term Debt
SP = Share Price
E = Earnings per Share
GP = Gross Profit
TS = Total Shares

FLIGHT SAFETY INTERNATIONAL (FSI) FEBRUARY 1996

- Book Value $= \frac{TA - IC - AL - SI}{S} = \frac{833 - 41 - 238}{31} = 17.8 \ (SP = \$53)$

- Debt/Equity Ratio $= \frac{AL}{SE} = \frac{238}{595} = 40\%$

- Net Current Asset Value/Share $= \frac{CA - CL}{S} = \frac{305 - 84}{31} = \frac{221}{31} = 7.1$

- Current Ratio $= \frac{CA}{CL} = \frac{305}{84} = 3.6$

- Net Quick Asset Value/Share $= \frac{CA - I - CL}{S} = \frac{305 - 8.7 - 84}{31} = \frac{212.3}{31} = 6.8$

- Quick Ratio $= \frac{CA - I}{CL} = \frac{305 - 8.7}{84} = 3.5$

- Net Net Current Assets/Share $= \frac{CA - CL - LTD}{S} = \frac{305 - 84 - 38}{31} = 5.1$

- Price/Earnings Ratio $= \frac{SP}{E} = \frac{53}{2.7} = 19.8$

- Profit Margin $= \frac{GP}{TS} = \frac{61}{157} = 39\%$

- Intrinsic Value $= E(2r + 8.5) \times \frac{4.4}{Y} = 2.7(20 + 8.5) \times \frac{4.4}{6} = \$56.4$

TA = Total Assets	833
IC = Intangible Assets	41
AL = All Liabilities	238
SI = Stock Issues	0
S = Number of Common Shares Outstanding	31
SE = Total Shareholders Equity	595
CA = Current Assets	305
CL = Current Liabilities	84
I = Inventory	8.7
LTD = Long-Term Debt	38
SP = Share Price	53
E = Earnings per Share	2.7

GP = Gross Profit   61
TS = Total Sales   157
r = Expected Earnings Growth Rate   10%
Y = Current Yield on AAA-Rated Corp. Bonds   6%

Identifying Growth in the Income Statement

That's the only growth rate that really counts: earnings.[1]

PETER LYNCH

S trong assets, as argued in Chapter 2, are essential because they ensure that a company will be around awhile to generate earnings. It is earnings, say Graham and Dodd, that drive share price growth:

> Stocks sell on earnings and dividends and not on cash-asset values—unless distribution of these cash assets is in prospect.[2]

The concept is simple enough. A company should produce enough income to pay operating expenses, cover debt, pay a dividend obligation if there is one, and still have sufficient resources to plow back into the operation to nurture future earnings growth. Because investors expect to share in the expected earnings, they buy the stock. The increased demand for the shares drives the price higher. Earnings are the honey that attracts the bees—in this case, investors.

Just as value investors demand evidence of a company's stability, so too do they look for validation of earnings. Most often they rely on the past performance for that validation. "If a business has a lousy past record but bright prospects," said Charles Munger, Warren Buffett's partner in the management of Berkshire Hathaway Inc., "we are going to pass on the opportunity."[3]

It's not just high current and past earnings that count, Graham taught his students. He told them to look at the quality of earnings, the stability of earnings, and the "qualitative" factors surrounding the "quantitative" figures. Much of this information on the ebb and flow—the energy and activity—of a company is found on the income statement.

WHAT IS THE INCOME STATEMENT?

The income statement often is called the profit and loss statement, or more familiarly, the P&L. (It would make more sense to call it a profit *or* loss statement, since each statement ends in one or the other, not both.) The P&L is divided into two main sections, revenues and expenses—and in the case of some companies, retained earnings. (When there are earnings to retain some companies list them along with dividends on the balance sheet.)

Within the revenue category are sales figures for the company's products or services, profits from the sale of an asset such as real estate or an operating division, and income earned from investments. Expenses include the cost of producing the goods or services, overhead expenses, depreciation, research and development costs, taxes, and other costs of doing business.

Graham had deep-seated misgivings about P&L numbers because he felt there were so many ways to shift, shuffle, hide, or embellish earnings. This was fertile ground for his satirical "experimental accounting laboratory." The treatment of nonrecurring profits or losses, operations of subsidiaries or affiliates, and depreciation and reserves was especially bothersome.

AN INVESTOR'S VIEW OF EARNINGS

When studying the income statement, look at the earnings from three points of view:

- *Accounting.* Are these true earnings? Do the numbers accurately and fairly represent the condition of the business?
- *Business.* What do these earnings imply as to future earnings of the company? Does the statement reflect a dynamic, growing entity?
- *Investment.* How can we use this information to evaluate share price?

An investor need not enroll in an auditing class to learn to read an income statement. Familiarity with the concepts introduced in this chapter will suffice.

But first, some perspective. When problems exist in an income statement, they tend to distort earnings only in a single year, or over a short period of time. To even out these short-term distortions, use average share price, annual earnings, and other numbers over a span of 7 to 10 years. "Averaging" establishes typical numbers for the company. The longer the time included in the average, the better.

FLASH PROFITS

Any one-time event that impacts earnings, such as a gain from the sale of an asset or a one-time loss resulting from a catastrophic event or the write-off of a potential debt, should be lifted out of the earnings figures and set to one side. These occurrences should be recognized for what they are and judged accordingly. They are in no way indicative of the outlook for future earnings.

A one-time sale of assets tends to make overall corporate profits look better in the year it occurs. Yet the sale, Graham pointed out, decreases the total assets of the company. There is no real gain unless the money is used for one of the following:

- Restore the asset base
- Reduce debt
- Contribute substantially to future earnings

In an established, well-managed company, daily operations finance themselves with cyclical shortfalls covered by short-term borrowing, so never should a one-time gain be used to cover ordinary expenses.

TAKING A HIT

Corporate accountants write off or write down items under several sets of circumstances. They may write a debt off the books that they are convinced will never be collected. They may mark down the value of an asset that is no longer worth what it once was. Excessive write-offs in one year can, in some circumstances, lead to greater than normal profits in the next. It's an old management trick to take all write-offs or write-downs during a period when earnings aren't looking so good anyway. The company decides to load all the bad news into one accounting period. Not only is it better psychologically to have one truly terrible period rather than several fairly bad ones, but the contrast between the bad quarter or year and the subsequent good one appears dramatic.

This jump in earnings thrills the investing public (the company did lousy last year, but look how it's come around!) But again, the better earnings may turn out to be a brief aberration. The following year the company's earnings fall back into the old ways.

Yet, done frankly and for the right reasons, write-downs may lead to real and long-lasting improvement in earnings. They make a difference when the company is saying: "This was a problem; we've faced up to it. The adjustment will allow the income statement to accurately reflect the condition of our company in the years ahead."

For alert investors, losses or gains that result from a single episode can be a boon. If other investors overreact to the news in either a positive or negative way, it may create a chance to buy or sell at an advantageous price.

CORPORATE TAXES

Back in the 1940s Graham suggested that to ensure that management is honest about earnings, corporations should make income tax statements available to investors upon request. If the company paid taxes on income, then it is genuine income. If the company didn't, there must be a logical reason, such as a tax write-off or the use of some type of tax credit. Corporate taxes have become progressively complex over the years, and only the most dedicated investors—and ones with a lot of time to kill—would care to pore over corporate tax statements.

Fortunately, many corporations now include summary tax information in their annual reports to shareholders. Many investor information services also supply simplified income tax information in their stock reports. Reporting of earnings on an after-tax basis is standard practice. In the end, says Peter Lynch, the "real bottom line" is profits after taxes.[4]

Some value investors interpret after-tax earnings as intrinsic value. "Let's say we have a small company that produces a widget and there are 100 shares outstanding. The $1000 invested in the company nets on the average $100 after taxes. The stock has an intrinsic value of $10 per share," writes investment manager Charles Brandes.[5]

INCOME THAT KEEPS COMING IN

If past earnings are to have any meaning to investors, there must be an inherent permanence to the earning power. Earnings can be cyclical, or even inconsistent, and still have some permanence. The largest U.S. automobile companies—General Motors, Ford, and Chrysler—have notoriously cyclical results; yet they've managed to keep up an ongoing business over many years.

Graham considered a company to have stable earnings when (1) earnings doubled in the most recent 10 years and (2) earnings declined by no more than 5 percent no more than twice in the past 10 years. Another approach to measuring stability is to compare one period of earnings with an earlier period. At Chrysler, for example, earnings per share nearly doubled in the 10-year period 1984–1994:

Stability is assessed by the trend of per-share earnings over a ten-year period, compared to the average of the most recent three years. No decline represents 100 percent stability.[6]

CHRYSLER EARNINGS PER SHARE, 1984–1994

Year	1984	1985	1986	1987	1988	1989	1990	1991	1992	1993	1994
Earnings per share	5.22	6.25	6.31	5.90	5.08	1.36	0.30	-2.7	1.38	6.77	10.1

10-year average = $4.95
3-year average = $6.08
1994 book value = $46.65 per share
1995 trading range = $38.25 to $58.13 per share

PROFITABILITY

Profitability can be measured in several ways, wrote Graham. His favorite was the ratio of operating income to sales as an indication of comparative weakness or strength. When Standard & Poor's stock reports include "operating income as a percentage of revenue" or Value Line details "profit margins," they also are presenting information on profitability. These are measures of cost control, efficiency, and competitiveness.

The best investment is often a company with a low profit margin relative to the rest of its industry, but with a strong likelihood that management is about to substantially improve future profit margins—a turnaround or a restructured company.

$$\text{Profit margin} = \frac{\text{gross profit}}{\text{net sales}}$$

This formula results in a ratio. To express profit margin as a percentage, multiply the result by 100. There are several other ways of calculating profit margin, but this is one of the easiest. Ideal profit margins vary from industry to industry.

The relationship between profit margin and share price performance is direct. When profit margin is low, share price often is too. For example, at Atlantic Richfield (Arco) 1984 operating income as a percentage of revenues was 17.2 percent, well under Arco's 10-year average of 23.5 percent. In 1985 the company's shares traded at a low of $42 and a high of $67.50. The operating margins began to rise and so did share price, until the price reached a high of $142.50 in 1990. That year the profit margin began to slip again, and by 1994 the company's operating income as a percentage of revenues was back to 17.4 percent and share price declined to $92.50. In 1994 and 1995 Arco restructured itself and improved its profit margin again, and by mid-1995 the share price lifted to around $114.

RETAINED EARNINGS

A company adds up its income, subtracts its expenses, and pays any dividends due; what is left becomes retained earnings. These are undistributed profits.

The retained earnings statement is a reconciliation of beginning and ending balances—an accumulation of undistributed profits over the years. That is why some companies place the retained earnings statement on the balance sheet rather than on the P&L. Wherever they are found, Graham said, undistributed profits are central to the process of investment growth:

ATTRIBUTES OF A COMMON STOCK

Common stocks have one important investment characteristic and one important speculative characteristic. Their investment value and average market price tend to increase irregularly but persistently over the decades, as their net worth builds up through the reinvestment of undistributed earnings.[7]

The speculative feature is no mystery. It is the tendency toward excessive and irrational price fluctuations as investors (in Graham's words) "give way to hope, fear, and greed."

If earnings are the honey that attracts investors, retained earnings are the hive around which swarms a certain amount of hope and greed. Corporate raiders in particular love to find a company with a loaded beehive.

There is a legitimate dispute over how much retained earnings are adequate, and at what level a company should let loose of some cash and distribute it to shareholders. Overall, retained earnings, like the payment of dividends, deliver a powerful message: the company generates more cash than it needs for the operation of the business. That's exactly what a good investment should do. These earnings, over and above total expenses and taxes, drive the share price higher.

IN *WATER WORLD* THEY ARE CALLED "SMOKERS"

In recent years, strong cash reserves have provoked takeover bids from corporate marauders who, like the wicked pirates in the movie *Water World*, want to flush out any riches that others may be hoarding. In

Water World survivors of global warming are fighting for dominance in a world where basic necessities have become scarce. But what about corporate raiders? Are they liberators of cash for shareholders or are they destroyers of American business, interested only in their own personal enrichment?

In the case of the Chrysler takeover attempt in April 1995, the raiders planned to use cash reserves to help finance their purchase, a tactic that often sucks the strength from a company. Former Chrysler chairman Lee Iacocca and corporate investor Kirk Kerkorian launched the unsolicited $20.8 billion, $55-per-share offer for Chrysler at a time when shares were trading as low as $38.25. The raiders planned a leveraged buyout using $2 billion in Chrysler shares already owned by Kerkorian, $12 to $13 billion in borrowed money, and $5.5 billion from Chrysler's own $7.6 billion cash reserves.

Management launched a furious defense, saying that Chrysler needed the cash to cover the next down cycle of the automobile manufacturing business. Shareholders and the bankers were chary of Kerkorian and Iacocca's plan to "devour Chrysler's seed corn," and did not get behind it. The honey drew the bees, but in this case the aggressor bees were unable to capture the hive.

HOW MUCH OF A GOOD THING?

While it's easy to describe the raiders as greedy, Graham, a quiet-spoken and gentlemanly person, didn't always see it that way. He was critical of amassing huge cash reserves within a business unless the company had a genuine future use for the funds. While a certain, calculable amount of reserves are necessary to finance growth, guard against bad luck or down cycles, cover the settlement of a lawsuit, or eventually replace some important asset, Graham argued, there is a limit to that need. The purpose of business is to earn profits for its owners. Owners are entitled to access to profits.

If earnings are retained, Graham persisted in his argument, they'd better be used intelligently.

Probably the greatest retainer of earnings of all time is Berkshire Hathaway, which keeps and reinvests all its earnings. (This certainly resolves Warren Buffett's tax problems—leaving most of his net worth on paper.) Berkshire's 23 percent return on shareholder equity is almost double that of American industry, and Buffett says he will continue to hoard earnings so as long as a dollar of retained earnings translates to no less than a dollar of increased shareholder value. In his case, investors are inclined to let him have his way.

DILUTION OF EARNINGS

One last reminder before moving on to the task of interpreting the meaning of earnings to investors. When considering a company's earnings per share history, make certain the numbers are adjusted for changes in capitalization; that is, work from fully diluted numbers. Be sure that all shares that have been authorized for issuance by the board of directors are added into the number of shares outstanding. Newly issued shares, split shares, and shelf registration (shares sitting in the company's vault but not yet issued) must be put in the pot.

This admonition applies not only to the most current earnings but to any earnings from the past that are used for comparison. The easiest way to make the adjustment when new shares are authorized is to work backward. Compute earlier earnings as if the new shares, rights, warrants, privileges, options, and so on already have been exercised. Corresponding changes should be made to book value and current asset value per share.

Fortunately, most companies include adjustments for shareholders in their financial statements, reporting figures on a fully diluted basis. But sometimes not. Several years ago a small California company released its financial report, which showed a marked increase in earnings from the year earlier. A closer look showed that a one-time sale of assets boosted earnings. Additionally, the previous year's earnings per share had been reported on a fully diluted basis, but the current earnings were not, making them seem stronger.

Surprise! About 6 months later it became obvious that the company was in bad trouble. Shareholders brought suit against the board for presenting misleading information. While such subterfuge should not take place, it does and this is why shareholders must be wide awake.

THE INTRINSIC VALUE FORMULA

If the intrinsic value is based on a company's future worth to an owner, and the future worth depends on future earnings, two important questions arise.

- How much should an investor pay for earnings?
- Is there a reliable way to forecast future earnings?

Graham invented a formula for determining intrinsic value using earnings in relation to AAA bond ratings. Few investors use it today, but it is interesting to study. When you are sitting on the fence about the worth of an investment, it can be used as yet another check on value.

In Graham's formula, E represents the company's earnings per share; r is the expected earnings growth rate; and Y the current yield on AAA corporate bonds. The number 8.5, Graham believed, is the correct price-to-earnings multiple for a company with no growth. P/E ratios have risen in recent years, perhaps making 15 to 20 a more appropriate number, but a conservative investor will continue to use a low multiplier.

$$\text{Intrinsic value} = E\,(2r + 8.5) \times 4.4/Y$$

Before accepting this formula too enthusiastically, you might reflect on Warren Buffett's response when asked about it. "I never use formulas like that. I never thought Ben was at his best when he worked with formulas either," he said with a chuckle.[8]

THE P/E RATIO

It is customary to study the price in relation to earnings, or the price-to-earnings ratio, as an indication of a company's earning power. When the price-to-earnings ratio is high, it is a sign that investors think earnings will be high; when the P/E is low, expectations are likewise.

$$\text{P/E ratio} = \frac{\text{Price}}{\text{past four quarters' per share earnings}}$$

A company with earnings of \$2 per share selling at \$20 has a P/E of 10. It is selling at 10 times earnings. The *trailing* P/E is based on last year's earnings. The *leading* P/E is based on estimated future earnings. Like most other financial ratios, a company's P/E is most meaningful when it is compared against previous years.

Though Graham placed much importance on well-documented earnings and accorded due respect to the P/E ratio as an investment tool, he considered the method far from perfect:

> The whole idea of basing the value upon current earnings seems inherently absurd, since we know that the current earnings are constantly changing. And whether the multiplier should be ten or fifteen or thirty would seem at bottom a matter of purely arbitrary choice.[9]

Not to toss out multiples altogether, Graham and Dodd said P/E ratios should be considered in context:

- Based upon a conservative or investment valuation of common stock, as opposed to speculation
- In terms of the significance of (1) capital structure and (2) source of income
- In light of unusual elements in the balance sheet that affect the earnings picture

Basically, the P/E of a desirable stock purchase should be below average for all stocks. It also should be below its own past P/E ratio. Graham liked to buy stocks with a multiple of no more than 7 to 10 times earnings. Conservative investors who can put less time and effort into their stock portfolios often must accept a higher P/E to achieve safety. Graham told defensive investors to shun stocks with a P/E above 20 times the past year's earnings or 25 times the average earnings of the previous 7 years:

> It is the essence of our viewpoint that some moderate upper limit must in every case be placed on the multiplier in order to stay within the conservative valuation. We would suggest that about 20 times average earnings is as high a price as can be paid in an investment purchase of common stock.[10]

THE UPPER LIMITS OF SHARE PRICE

The P/E also can be used to establish a cap on intrinsic value. While asset values set the lowest level for estimating intrinsic value, the P/E can serve as an upper limit. The price-to-earnings ratio establishes the maximum amount an investor should pay for earnings. If the investor decides that the appropriate price-to-earnings ratio for a stock is 10, the share price paid should be no more than 10 times most recent yearly earnings.

It is not wrong to pay more, Graham and Dodd noted; it is simply that doing so enters the realm of speculation. Since young, rapidly expanding companies generally trade at a P/E of 20 to 25 or above, Graham usually avoided them, which was one reason he never invested in IBM, though he used and was impressed by IBM's products early in his career.

A PRICEY P/E

A company may be selling at an exceptionally high P/E because it is considered to have remarkably good prospects for growth. But again, run a check. Multiply the current earnings by the P/E ratio, then make the typical adjustments for inflation 10 years down the road. Does the 10-year-out share price sound reasonable? No matter how high the quality of the car you are looking at, there is a price at which it is no longer worth buying. No matter how junky a car is, there is a price at which it is a bargain. Stocks are no different.

Popular technology stocks sometimes sell at multiples as high as 30, 40, or 50 times the past 12 months' earnings per share. Some stocks with high multiples work out, but investors who consistently buy high-multiple stocks are likely to lose money in the long run. Often, the highest multiples are present in a bull market, observed Graham and Dodd, which increases the risk:

It is a truism to say that the more impressive the record and the more promising the prospects of stability and growth, the more liberally the per-share earnings should be valued, subject always to our principle that a multiplier higher than about 20 (i.e., "earnings basis" of less than 5 percent) will carry the issue out of the investment range."

A SUBNORMAL P/E

When a stock is selling at a P/E significantly lower than that of its competitors, an investor will want to know why. A low P/E does not necessarily mean higher risk, though the company should be studied with that possibility in mind. The low P/E stock may be selected anyway if, for example, it is a cyclical stock at a low in its cycle. Cyclical stocks—automobile manufacturers are the most notorious among them—periodically develop fire-sale P/E ratios. Other out-of-favor stocks also can drop to surprisingly low P/Es. When investors Kerkorian and Iacocca made their hostile move on Chrysler, the auto company was selling at a multiple of 4. Even the day after the $55-per-share takeover offer, when Chrysler shares rose to $48.75, the stock's P/E was less than 6.

On the other hand, if a stock is cheap in terms of its multiple for a troubling reason, such as pending depletion of oil or mineral reserves or a patent expiration, the value investor may want to shop elsewhere.

EARNINGS, SALES, AND FUTURE GROWTH

The goal of the value investor is to identify companies with a solid financial base that are growing at a faster rate (in terms of sales and earnings) than both their competitors and the economy in general. All things being equal, share price is likely to increase in value at about the same rate that sales grow. For dominant companies in major industries, an investor will want a sales growth rate of 5 to 7 percent. Within a portfolio, look for an overall sales growth rate of at least 10 percent annually.

Earnings need not rise every year. Almost all industries operate in cycles, and any company can suffer a temporary setback. But investors should be wary when a company's earnings and sales are erratic without explanation or when sales and earnings are slowly sinking and the company is not taking corrective action.

TRENDS

As noted earlier, Graham warned against judging a company on current earnings, versus long-term average earnings:

> This is the most important difference between a privately held company and a public corporation. A private business might easily earn twice as much in a boom year as in poor times, but its owner would never think of correspondingly marking up or down the value of his capital investment.[12]

Again, evaluate the earnings trend by figuring the P/E on the basis of a 10-year average of both earnings and share price. Note the direction. If P/E ratios in the most recent years are significantly and increasingly higher than the 10-year average, a stock may very well be worth more than its longer-term average might suggest. If the P/E trend is lackluster or downward, the stock may well be worth less than its 10-year earnings average would indicate. Most trends can be established in a similar way.

EARNINGS TREND

| | Earnings per Share ($) in Successive Year | | | | | | | | |
COMPANY	1ST	2ND	3RD	4TH	5TH	6TH	7TH	7-YEAR AVERAGE	TREND
A	1	2	3	4	5	6	7	4	Excellent
B	7	7	7	7	7	7	7	7	Neutral
C	13	12	11	10	9	8	7	10	Bad

Source: *Security Analysis* (New York: McGraw-Hill, 1940), p. 512

READING TEA LEAVES

Even though a record of increasing earnings and profits is a favorable sign, Graham and Dodd looked askance at projections:

> While a trend shown in the past is a fact, a "future trend" is only an assumption. The past, or even careful projections, can be seen as only a "rough index" to the future.[13]

More than five decades have passed since those words were said, and Buffett still agrees. "I have no use whatsoever for projections or forecasts. They create an illusion of apparent precision. The more meticulous they are, the more concerned you should be. We never look at projections but we care very much about, and look very deeply, at track records. If a company has a lousy track record but a very bright future, we will miss the opportunity," explained Buffett.

Charlie Munger, Buffett's partner, added that in his opinion projections do more harm than good. "They are put together by people who have an interest in a particular outcome, have a subconscious bias, and its apparent precision makes it fallacious. They remind me of Mark Twain's saying, 'A mine is a hole in the ground owned by a liar.' Projections in America are often a lie, although not an intentional one, but the worst kind because the forecaster often believes them himself."[14]

MAKING EARNINGS GROW

It is only rational, however, to have an opinion on future growth. Otherwise, how could you ever choose a stock? When forming that opinion, back up quantitative information with qualitative factors. For example, ask what management is doing to make a positive impact on earnings.

According to Peter Lynch, "There are five basic ways a company can increase earnings: reduce costs; raise prices; expand into new markets; sell more of its products to the old markets; or revitalize, close or otherwise dispose of a losing operation.[15] When management is enacting growth-promoting activities, earnings may be temporarily flat. They often soon take a giant step up.

An article in *Money* magazine reminds us that Graham saw "a vulnerability in a high growth rate and in high returns on capital—and the two normally go together." So what's there to worry about in good earnings? Exceptionally high earnings often attract rough competitors. The good part is that high earnings lure enthusiastic new investors, who often bid the share into the stratosphere.[16]

GROWTH STOCKS

There is a sometimes useless delineation between value investors and growth investors. By the false reckoning of some investment counselors, value investors don't buy growth stocks. Of course they do. How else could value investors achieve such high investment returns? The argument is a matter of semantics. Value investors would buy *only* growth companies if they could be sure which ones *were* growth companies. What, after all, is a growth stock? When the term implies a speculative venture, value investors bow out. A true value investment is one that has enormous growth potential with limited downside risk.

The riskier so-called growth stocks ordinarily are young companies, some of which produce little or no earnings. Frequently they are in a new industry that has many initial competitors. The field of competitors will be reduced as time passes, and the difficulty lies in spotting the Ford versus the Packard; the Hewlett-Packard versus the Kaypro; the Price/Costco versus dozens of upstart warehouse stores.

According to Graham, a growth stock should double its per share earnings in 10 years—that is, increase earnings at a compound annual rate of over 7.1 percent. To do so, a growth stock's sales should be continually higher than sales in the early years:

> The investor who can successfully identify such "growth companies" *when their shares are available at reasonable prices* is certain to do superlatively well with his capital.[17]

GROWTH STRATEGY

The search for maximum portfolio growth will be addressed in future chapters. Suffice it to say at this point that there are investors who can and should invest the time and effort to create a super high-growth portfolio.

Although it will require greater effort in selection and maintenance, a high-performance portfolio can be achieved while abiding by the commandments of value. Any appearance of higher risk must be well understood and accounted for in the share price. Pushing the limit, say Graham and Dodd, is a game for the strong-minded and daring individual.[18]

WITHOUT EARNINGS, NOTHING TO MEASURE

Graham was suspicious of "hot" or fast-growth stocks because their promise relies on the prediction of ever-increasing future earnings with little historical evidence that the company can consistently produce ever-rising future earnings. He warned the growth stock investor to seek two things:

- Assurance that growth will continue
- Assurance that the investor isn't paying too high a price for future growth

Many high-tech, bio-tech or other emerging technology companies operate more like venture capital operations. Venture capitalists demand guarantees of high returns because the risk is high that earnings will be slow in arriving, or will never materialize at all. The venture capitalist is betting on a technology and the talent to put that technology into use. Venture capital investment is best practiced by those who know a particular industry extremely well.

Peter Lynch warns investors to be especially careful with companies in formation. "Wait for the earnings," he cautions. Though Lynch has done very well with some initial public offerings in particular (he was an original investor in Federal Express), "I'd say three out of four have been long-term disappointments."[19]

CONCLUSION

Toward the end of his life Graham spent many hours looking for one simple criterion on which to base stock purchases. His focus turned to earnings. "My research indicates that the best results come from simple earnings criterions," he told one reporter. However, the research he spoke of was never thoroughly tested. His multiple criteria for selecting investment-quality stocks have remained the most reliable.[20]

What makes an "investment-quality stock"?

• Financial condition is conservative and working capital position is strong.

• Earnings are reasonably stable, allowing for business conditions that fluctuate over a 10-year period.

• Average earnings bear a satisfactory ratio to market price.

As investors become more familiar with these guidelines, they follow them easily and automatically—or so it seems.

Buffett and his partner, Charlie Munger, say they don't sweat over formal rules or procedures when trying to determine if a stock has growth potential. Once, when someone subpoenaed Berkshire's staff papers on an acquisition, they explained, "Not only did we not have the papers, we didn't have the staff."[21]

For those of us with less talent and experience than Buffett and Munger, however, it is acceptable to work out a portfolio plan and run a tally of a stock's pluses and minuses. More about how to do that in the next two chapters.

IN THE MEANTIME, REMEMBER

Quantitative data are useful only to the extent that they are supported by a qualitative survey of the enterprise.[22]

• The companies with the best investment potential are consistently profitable.

• Earnings should trend upward.

• The P/E ratio should be low compared with those of other companies in the same industry.

- The P/E ratio establishes the upper share price limit on intrinsic value.
- Earnings and other estimates should err on the side of understatement. That, in itself, makes for a margin of safety.

4

Management's Role

Corporations are in law the mere creatures and property of the stockholders who own them; the officers are only the paid employees of the stockholders; the directors, however chosen, are virtually trustees, whose legal duty is to act solely in behalf of the owners of the business.[1]

GRAHAM AND DODD

hen Graham and Dodd wrote the passage above, shareholder ownership was little more than a legal concept. Shareholders were seen mostly as lenders of capital. It was still accepted practice for corporate managers to run public companies as if they were the sole owners. Their instruction to shareholders, unless they owned a very large number of shares, was blunt: "If you don't like the way we run the company, you can vote with your feet. Sell your shares and move along." Graham and Dodd impaled on a sharpened spear the quivering friction between shareholders and corporate management:

A private employer hires only men he can trust, but he does not let these men fix their own salaries or decide how much capital he should place or leave in the business.[2]

There is an inherent conflict in the structure of public corporations, Graham believed, which requires the company's owners (the shareholders) to place extraordinary power in the hands of those who run the company—the chief executive officer, in particular.

SAVED BY THE CEO

One of the few positions of omnipotence in the world today is that of chief executive officer of a major corporation. The CEO is self-selected by scoring victories in a series of career battles. He or she is nominated by an inside group and elected in a process that could never hope to pass as democratic. The CEO answers to a board of directors, but if the CEO has been around more than a few years, the board is made up of people of the executive's own choosing. All too often the board merely rubber-stamps the CEO's own proposals.

Yet there is little doubt that the management team, assembled and orchestrated by the chief executive, is key to the success of a company. But how that role should be played out, how it should be rewarded, and how it should be evaluated keeps corporate gadflies sleepless at night.

At the 1988 annual meeting of Capital Cities/ABC in Phoenix, Warren Buffett donned a Salvation Army uniform, tooted on a tin horn, and serenaded the company's chairman, Thomas Murphy. "What a friend I have in Murphy," Buffett crooned. Thus far there is no insider intelligence regarding the song that Buffett sang in 1995 when Cap Cities/ABC was sold to the Walt Disney Co., delivering to Berkshire Hathaway a 600 percent profit in 10 years. There is no question that Buffett appreciated Murphy's good work, but for a value investor there's more to the story than that.

Value investors start with the business itself—its fundamentals— then evaluate the impact of management as an added element. The business is like a vehicle and management is the driver. No matter how good a driver is, she won't have much luck jockeying a low-slung Honda Civic through the sands of the Sahara Desert.

CHOOSE A TERRIFIC BUSINESS

"If you have to choose between terrific management and a terrific business, choose the terrific business," says Warren Buffett.[3]

Despite Graham's admonition that there is potential value even in badly managed companies, Buffett will not buy shares in a company unless there is management in place that he trusts. He isn't in the business of managing businesses, and he isn't willing to invest the time for management troubles to work themselves out. (For further discussion on companies in dire straits, turn to Chapter 9.)

"If the company cannot be expected to stand on its own two feet for years after the ink is dry, we would not be interested," Buffett said.[4]

A FEUDAL SYSTEM BASED ON HONOR

Buffett's ideal business? He likes "wonderful castles, surrounded by deep, dangerous moats, where the leader inside is an honest and decent person."[5] It is interesting that the words "honest and decent" are so important in Buffett's definition that they get top billing at the end of the sentence. Where is the world "able"? Unless the lord of the castle is honest and decent in his treatment of his various constituents (investors included), it little matters how able he is.

Deciding if the leadership is principled is a qualitative or value judgment that many investors aren't in a position to make. They may never get to meet the CEO in person or even indirectly. And even if they do, the charisma so often found in such leaders can lead investors astray.

MILKING THE CASH COW

It has happened that increased earnings have not benefited shareholders because corporate managers have diverted the gains into their own pocketbooks. The price of shareholdership, like that of living in a democracy, is constant vigilance. It behooves investors to keep up with the news, check out rumors, and generally stay well informed about the companies they own and the people who run them.

"Run from corporate managers more concerned with perquisites, golden parachutes, bonuses, and excessively high salaries in relation to the return to shareholders," advises Charles Brandes, director of Brandes Investment Partners.[6]

Many financial magazines and newspapers publish stories and charts on the highest-paid executives, analyzing their compensation in relation to the company's performance. Shareholders should peruse the corporate literature—the proxy statement, in particular—for management compensation figures. Beware of special loans to management or other arrangements that seem preferential or out of line.

Executive compensation is a thorny issue. Many executives feel that the larger the company they run, the larger their salary should be. This motivates a significant number of acquisitions and takeovers that otherwise would not happen. Other executives feel their compensation should be tied to the rate of return they achieve for shareholders. The higher the return, the higher the bonus. The correct answer is that both factors should influence salary. It does seem wrong, however, that the return in any single year should activate a bonus. Most competent accountants can arrange for an exceptional yearly return from time to time. Rather, like earnings, dividends, and other quantitative factors, CEOs should be compensated on the average return over at least a 5-year period. Executives should not receive bonuses for performance unless they outperform their industry as a whole in such specific areas as earnings per share, return on equity, and profit margins. Otherwise, top management is given extra salary for being merely average.

MANAGERS WHO THINK LIKE OWNERS

Buffett and his partner, Charlie Munger, run Berkshire Hathaway according to "owner-related business principles," and they look for companies that are managed in the same way. The first principle is that though Berkshire's form is corporate, "our attitude is partnership." It is also significant that Buffett and Munger have their personal wealth tied up in Berkshire. "We eat our own cooking," they tell shareholders.[7]

Charles Brandes likes to find companies where management not only thinks like an owner but, like Buffett and Munger, has staked out a substantial ownership position. "If a president owns 20 percent or more of the shares outstanding, then we both want the same thing—increased share price. Managers tied only by salary and benefits aren't rowing the same boat as shareholders."[8]

Dominant owners who serve on the board of directors also can exert great control over management. Companies like General Dynamics, Du Pont, Kellogg, and The Times Mirror Company have dominant owners. Management has no trouble putting a face to the intangible concept of "shareholder."

QUALITATIVE FACTORS

There are other important qualitative factors to be considered when evaluating management. Among them are the company's market share (industry leaders are preferred to those in fourth place or lower), its products, and its efficiency in making those products. Ordinarily, for the best growth in a mature company, the investor looks for new product development. These new products can make an old company's shares act like those of a smaller, emerging company.

Some investors want a company to be adequately diversified. Diversification may make sense on the face of it, but if a company is already involved in one of the most profitable businesses ever, why diversify into less profitable areas? What good can that do for the bottom line?

Think of Coca Cola. The company's growth slowed during the time it tried to diversify by introducing new products. New Coca Cola, a highly publicized beverage, was an embarrassing failure. The more the company concentrates on "old Coke" and introducing the traditional Coca Cola to new markets, the faster it grows.

Profitability, even if it evolves from a nontraditional approach, is the ultimate measure of good management. If management is performing, Graham and Dodd say, it will be reflected in the financial statements:

> The most convincing proof of capable management lies in a superior comparative record over a period of time. But this brings us back to the quantitative data.[9]

THE QUANT WANTS EVIDENCE

"A value standpoint requires that the investor pay only for what is seen, not what is hoped," reminds Brandes.[10] There are several balance sheet and income statement measures of management performance. The three most common are:

- *Rate of company growth.* Examine sales trends and profit trends.
- *Profit margin before taxes.* Are costs being controlled?
- *Earnings on invested capital.* The single most important mark of good management is high earnings on invested capital. It is the element that is common to all businesses, whether they be large or small; involved in manufacturing or services; privately or publicly controlled. The owners expect to make money.

$$\text{Return on invested capital} = \frac{\text{net income + interest expense}}{\text{total capitalization}}$$

The average return on invested capital is about 12 to 13 percent. Analysts consider anything between 12 and 25 percent after taxes to be a superior showing.

MANAGEMENT'S RELATIONSHIP TO SHARE PRICE

Corporate executives often complain that the gyrations of their company's share price confounds them; they feel they have little control over it. On a day-to-day fluctuation basis, this may very well be true. In the short term, the market jives to its own tune. Though it sometimes takes the market an agonizingly long time, eventually it does recognize the work of good management and reward that effort by trading the price up.

Graham said the competence of management is reflected in the "average" market price and the long-term price trend:

Good managements produce a good average market price, and bad managements produce bad market prices.[11]

Furthermore, it is management's responsibility to be concerned about share price:

It is at least as important to the stockholders that they be able to obtain a fair price for their share as it is that the dividends, earnings and assets be conserved and increased. It follows that the responsibility of management to act in the interest of their shareholders includes the obligation to prevent—in so far as they are able—the establishment of either absurdly high or unduly low prices for their securities.[12]

TO SCHMOOZE OR NOT TO SCHMOOZE

Charles Brandes recommends examining a company's economic value in relationship to its price; then, if you are satisfied with the numbers, appraise the people in charge. If you have questions regarding factual matters, put in a call to the chief executive or the chief financial officer. If that fails, contact the company's investor relations department. "A lot of these guys are like the Maytag repairman—lonesome," notes Brandes. "They love to talk."[13]

For some investors, however, nothing replaces a visit to the company. Warren Buffett says that when he worked at Graham Newman in the mid-1950s his only grievance was that Graham didn't want him to call on companies or talk to management. Buffett thought he'd know a company better if he met the CEO in person, toured a plant or two, and generally got a feel for things. Peter Lynch started his career calling on companies to size them up for Fidelity Investments.

Whether to go on the road or not to go is a matter of personal style. Some investors feel they may be too easily dazzled by sweet-talking corporate executives. Graham himself felt that way. Nobody reaches the upper tier of corporate society without salesmanship skills. On the other hand, an observant investor may come up with a general sense of what the company is about.

Small investors may not get an open door if they call a company president, but they can attend an annual meeting. The way that shareholder meetings are run says a lot about a company.

THE ANATOMY OF AN ANNUAL MEETING

WD-40, maker of the ubiquitous all-purpose lubricant, for years held its annual meeting on the shop floor. Tables and chairs were unfolded on a bare cement slab among the tanks holding formula number WD-

40, for which the product was named. The message was "We're a simple, conservative company, and our annual meetings are the same."

WD-40 in recent years moved its shareholder meeting to a hotel, but it still is a refreshingly straightforward event. The board of directors sit at the front on a platform and take any and all questions from shareholders. No planting people in the audience to ask the right questions; no screening written questions so as to avoid embarrassing subjects. While WD-40 has had its challenges, it has maintained a reputation for respecting and rewarding shareholders.

Some shareholder meetings are rushed affairs that last just long enough to go through the motions of electing a board, approving an auditor, and passing management's proposals. Management in these cases does not seem to care much about talking or listening to shareholders in general.

Other companies hold carefully orchestrated, slick shows intended to impress those who attend but to squelch gadfly or other disgruntled shareholders. And no wonder. When shareholders are riled, an annual meeting can get nasty. One of the most raucous annual meetings in corporate history, unfortunately for management, was played live on national television following the 1989 *Exxon Valdez* oil spill in Alaska. Activist shareholders made their feelings known and demanded answers from an openly hostile and reticent management team.

At one such meeting of a now defunct San Diego savings and loan, a microphone was being passed around the audience and the chairman was answering questions. An irate shareholder captured the mike and delivered his own analysis of the company's financial position and its plans for the year ahead. He and other shareholders began shouting their complaints and demands at the board of directors. It was nearly 20 minutes of pandemonium before company employees recaptured the microphone and wrestled the meeting back under their own control. The rogue shareholders raised some vital issues. Within a few years the savings and loan empire descended into the hands of the Resolution Trust Corporation—the industry's regulatory undertaker.

Meetings like that of course are the exception. More often, management simply presents a case for being kept on board. Although shareholders usually are asked to sign in at corporate annual meetings, many companies will allow nonshareholder visitors. This is one opportunity to see corporate leaders face to face and get a sense of their enthusiasm about the future, their attitudes, and their abilities.

SHAREHOLDER RIGHTS

Value investors, who believe that shareholders are a company's owners, sometimes find themselves at odds with management, as Graham himself did. Kahn Brothers, a company that traces its ancestry directly to an early association with Graham, is well known for its shareholder versus management litigations. "Most shareholders are sheep and are reluctant to stand up and take action. We've been forced to act in order to defend ourselves and our clients," explains Alan Kahn.[14]

While Graham himself was not a particularly litigious person, he did encourage shareholders to exercise their ownership rights, though he had little faith that they actually would do so. Graham and Dodd described the typical U.S. stockholder as "the most docile and apathetic animal in captivity,"[15] and asserted:

> It is in the best interests of everyone if shareholders are better educated to their rights and are willing to exercise them.[16]

There are three common (though mistaken) assumptions that keep shareholders from being more assertive. Shareholders often believe that

- Management knows more about the business than stockholders do.
- Management has no responsibility for or interest in the share price.
- If stockholders are unhappy with management, they should sell their stock.

The first assumption is a half-truth, Graham claimed. Management may know the business, but that doesn't mean it will follow the best course for shareholders. If the earnings are used primarily to inflate management's own salaries and perks, to make ego-based acquisitions, or to simply sustain management's own position, it isn't so good. In recent years, there has been more shareholder activity than existed in Graham's early years on Wall Street. A flood of shareholder lawsuits beginning in the 1980s and expanding in the 1990s spurred the 1995 Congress to take action to protect corporations from their owners—the shareholders.

The second wrong assumption—that management has no involvement in share price—was discussed earlier. Avoid investing in companies when management holds this attitude.

The third assumption—that shareholders who are unhappy should sell—is exactly the kind of mind set that allows a self-serving management to keep its grip on corporate coffers. Shareholders of all kinds, many of them with health, religious, social, and investment-oriented agendas, are rejecting that notion.

Most shareholders today are aware that they have options other than selling their shares if they don't like a company's social, political, environmental, employee, or financial policies. Dialogues with management, shareholder proposals on the proxy statement, and individual and class action lawsuits have an impact. Yet attempting to influence management decisions or change corporate policy is time-consuming. It can detract from an investor's main objective—to make money. From an investment point of view, it makes more sense to study and understand management before a stock is purchased, and to find companies that are engaged in acceptable activities from the start.

CONCLUSION

Graham often told his students that when a good business has bad management, several things will happen. The first effect is that the stock price is likely to decline, sometimes to the point that the shares become an asset play. If the board of directors is doing its job, there may be a change of top management. If not, change will be forced on the company. The company may become a takeover target or, in the worst case, the company will fall into bankruptcy.

One of the most powerful polemics for shareholder rights appears in the 1940 edition of *Security Analysis*. Reduced to its essence, Graham and Dodd's message is as follows: It is the business of business to make money for its owners, and to pass that money along to the owners—in the form of increased dividends, growth of share price, or return of capital in some other way, such as a direct cash payout.[17]

IN THE MEANTIME, REMEMBER

- If faced with a choice between great management and a great business, pick the great business.
- Look for skinflint management. Are top executives financially prudent, even when it comes to their own salaries and benefits?
- Favor companies in which management has a large ownership stake.
- Look for growth in sales and profits and return on shareholder equity to confirm management's sense of responsibility.
- Defend your shareholder rights. After all, you own the company.

5

Building a Portfolio

We seek not to imitate the masters; rather, we seek what they sought.

WALT DISNEY COMPANY MISSION STATEMENT

In 1970 Benjamin Graham planned to write a revision of his classic investment book, *The Intelligent Investor*. He enlisted the help of his former acolyte and now friend, Warren Buffett. As the process of collaboration evolved, it became clear that they had different opinions about how to approach the market. Graham held to his concept of "defensive" investors and "enterprising" investors, distinctions Buffett believed were no longer functional. All investors, he thought, should be enterprising. Though the two men consulted and discussed various ideas that ended up in the book, and later Buffett wrote the preface and contributed a piece for the appendix, he never became a coauthor.

When investment advisers around the world talk about structuring a portfolio for the needs of individual investors, their advice generally falls into the "less" category or the "more" category. Those who have less money, less knowledge, and less time before they need to spend their money should take less risk. Those who have more money, more knowledge, and more time to recoup possible losses . . . you get the idea.

A CONTINUUM OF INTELLECTUAL ENERGY

Graham's defensive/enterprising concept didn't quite fall along the conventional more/less lines. Risk, to his way of thinking, was linked not to how much money an investor can afford to lose, but to how much work the investor can and will do:

> It has been an old and sound principle that those who cannot afford to take risks should be content with a relatively low return on their invested funds. From this there has developed the general notion that the rate of return which the investor should aim for is more or less proportionate to the degree of risk he is ready to run. Our view is different. The rate of return sought should be dependent, rather, on the amount of intelligent effort the investor is willing and able to bring to bear on his task.[1]

Defensive investors need a low-maintenance, extremely safe portfolio, whereas enterprising investors can actively monitor and manage their accounts. It is the intensity of management, rather than the additional risk, that creates the higher return.

Though Buffett believes that all investors need to bring a special enlightenment to contemporary markets, an argument can still be made in favor of Graham's two categories. Some investors are able to devote greater time and attention to their portfolios, and it logically follows that their returns may very well be higher. Yet a category of investor that is often overlooked today is the individual whose main focus in life is not on investments, but rather on a career or some other enterprise. That person should and can successfully manage his own stock portfolio, especially if he follows a defensive strategy. Even Buffett has a segment of Berkshire Hathaway's funds in a virtually permanent portfolio which requires little day-to-day oversight.

Some investors have been misled to believe that all value portfolios tend to be sluggish, low-energy animals.

PARABLE OF THE GROWTH FUND

In the summer of 1995 a young executive of a mutual fund company was discussing portfolio management with a business journalist, who happened to mention one of the principles of value investing in relation to portfolio strategy. "Oh well," the man said. "We're a growth mutual fund company you know. We're much more aggressive." Minutes before, the executive had been describing with pride the 15 to 18 percent (after costs) average annual return of some of the growth company's funds.

While this is an excellent return considering that many mutual funds don't beat the Dow, it is overshadowed by the performance of supposedly conservative value investors who—over 10 or more years—achieve annual returns ranging from 17 percent to 27 percent. Studies testing Graham's principles of buying low P/E ratio stocks (a P/E of around 6 is ideal, though not always possible) showed in various market stretches average annual returns of between 16.8 percent and 37 percent. Growth stocks sometimes accelerate in price faster than that, but unless corporate growth translates to a sustainable increase in share price, what benefit is that to investors?

Some investment writers accuse value practitioners of abandoning their principles when the investors' choices appear to be less than conservative. The writer may be confusing the concept of "conservative" with that of "conventional."

CONSERVATIVE IS AS CONSERVATIVE DOES

When he was just 35 years old and still running the Buffett Limited Partnership, Buffett expressed his own frustration over the definition of conservative investing. Apparently his critics were saying that BLP was less conservative than most mutual funds. "It is unquestionably true that the investment companies have their money more conventionally invested that we do," Buffett wrote. "To many people, conventionality is indistinguishable from conservatism."

This is wrong headed, insisted Buffett. "Truly conservative actions arise from intelligent hypotheses, correct facts, and sound reasoning. These qualities may lead to conventional acts, but there have been many times when they have led to unorthodoxy," he concluded.[2]

To search for undervalued stocks that personal research shows have some value not yet recognized by the investing public may seem both conventional and conservative to some, but the results often are neither. In this chapter we will investigate various approaches for those who consider themselves defensive investors, and those who see themselves as enterprising. But first we need to consider the broader guidelines for portfolio building.

GOALS

There may be as many investment goals as there are investors. Graham's teaching can be applied to virtually any investment objective. Those who prefer to defer taxes for as long as possible can buy and hold for the long term. Those who need current income can choose from a large number of dividend-paying securities, many of which also have a satisfactory record of share price growth. Investors who choose to avoid certain types of business activity—tobacco, alcohol, weapon, or abortion pill producers, for example—can quite easily overlay their goals on value investing principles. They will find numerous value-based securities that meet their investment objectives—in both ethical terms and financial terms. The principles are general; the choices are personal.

A SUITABLE RETURN

Graham told investors that they should approach investment activities with the right attitude—not only toward buying and selling securities, but in regard to their expectations. To expect too much or too little from a portfolio can put investors in the wrong frame of mind.

While greed can lead to bad decisions, it also is a mystery that some investors actively seek mediocrity. Index funds are sold to thousands of investors who then are relegated to losing what the market loses and gaining no more than what the market gains. Just as confusing, investment managers often are judged by whether or not they do as well as the Dow Jones Industrial Average (DJIA).

Investors who have taken the time and made the effort to study investing principles may not be satisfied merely to achieve what the Dow achieves. The index sometimes is dog-days lazy. In 1973 the Dow's total return was down 13.12 percent and in 1974 it dropped another 23.14 percent. At other times we're lucky if we can keep up with the DJIA: in 1975 the return on the Dow went up 44.4 percent.

Most of the time, however, the Dow's performance is just what it's described as—average. During the 4-year period between 1978 and 1982, for example, the DJIA appreciated a total of 28.6 percent, for a yearly average of 7.15 percent. Over the long haul, 9 percent to 10 percent a year is the typical return for stocks in general. (Fortunately, the stock market's long-term direction has been ever higher.)

It's easy to achieve the same performance as the Dow—merely buy equal dollar amounts of the 30 stocks that make up the DJIA. There also is a simple way to improve on the Dow's performance. Apply value investing principles to the Dow stocks only—choosing those that are undervalued and selling those that are overvalued—and keep enough money in bonds or cash to take advantage of stock market and interest rate hiccups. In his book *Beating the Dow*, Michael O'Higgins teaches investors similar methods.

So what is a reasonable expectation? Investors who do a good job on their portfolios should be getting a 12 percent to 15 percent return, compounded over time. This rate of return is well rooted in investing history.

"If people with either large or small capital would look upon trading in stocks as an attempt to get twelve per cent per annum on their money instead of fifty percent weekly, they would come out a good deal better in the long run," wrote Charles Dow at the turn of the century. "Everybody knows this in its application to his private business, but the man who is prudent and careful in carrying on a store, a factory or a real estate business seems to think that totally different methods should be employed in dealing with stocks. Nothing is further from the truth."[3]

Even Warren Buffett realistically aims at no more than 15 percent return on assets; anything else is frosting on the cake. Buffett's cake has had mountains of frosting, no doubt because he pays a lot of attention to his work. Even after years of experience and success, Buffett aims at a substantial margin of safety in the securities he buys.

DIVERSIFICATION

Diversification is one of the three foundations upon which Graham built his "margin of safety." Graham likens diversification to the arithmetic of roulette. If the reward for hitting the right number is low, the gambler's chance of losing money becomes greater only by playing more numbers. But if the reward for hitting the right number is high enough, rewards are greatly enhanced by choosing more numbers. This is another way of saying that the higher the possible reward, the greater good it does to diversify.

An investor who could spot winners accurately every time wouldn't need to diversify. Most investors are not that infallible; diversification offers the following advantages.

- It smooths out market bumps in terms of total return. Stocks do not rise and fall in lock step. The National Association of Investors Corporation calls this the Rule of Five. "The rule holds that one of five stocks will bump into unforeseen troubles, three will more or less hit targets, and one will do better by far than expected."[4]

- It allows flexibility when raising cash becomes necessary. An investor has more options when a sale becomes unavoidable, Graham said:

> The true investor scarcely ever is forced to sell his shares, and at all other times he is free to disregard the current price quotation.[5]

- It affords some protection against interest rate shifts and other conditions that affect share price. Every portfolio should include an interest-earning component as part of its diversification mix.

- It increases the chances of hitting what Peter Lynch calls a "ten-bagger." These are stocks that do so well they significantly lift the total return on the entire portfolio.

Graham's recommendations on this matter can be broken down into Diversification Rule Number One and Diversification Rule Number Two.

DIVERSIFICATION RULE NUMBER ONE

> My basic rule is that the investor should always have a minimum of 25 percent in bonds or bond equivalents, and another minimum of 25 percent in common stocks. He can divide the other 50 percent between the two, according to the varying stock and bond prices.[6]

One way to envision this diversification technique is to think of an Oriental abacus, an old-fashioned calculator that uses beads. At the left end of the abacus, one-fourth of the beads would represent investments in stocks. At the other end of the abacus, one-fourth of the beads would always represent bonds or some other interest-bearing investment with a guaranteed rate of return. The beads in the middle—50 percent of the total number of beads—would move left or right depending on market conditions. If there were plenty of bargain stocks to buy, most of the beads would be on the left. If good stocks were scarce or if exceptionally high rates were available on government securities, certificates of deposits, or other accounts with a guaranteed return, most of the middle beads would move to the right side of the abacus.

When in doubt, stocks should prevail. Even the most conservative investor should have a portfolio that is as strong as possible in stocks, Graham noted, for two reasons:

- Stocks offer the best protection against the eroding effects of inflation on money.
- Stocks historically provide higher average returns than other forms of investment.

At the same time, the most astute investors are comfortable with cash holdings. At his 1995 annual meeting, Buffett explained, "Cash is a residual. If we like something we will buy it. If we can't find outstanding value, we absolutely do not feel compelled to buy something just because we are holding cash."[7]

CASH, BONDS, AND EQUIVALENTS

Graham explained that bonds, bond equivalents, and cash serve the following purposes:

- As protection
- As a storehouse of value
- At times as a source of superior return—though usually those episodes are short-lived

Investing in government bonds, corporate bonds, and other interest-bearing securities is a sophisticated discipline in and of itself. Fixed-income investing is further influenced by the introduction in the past 20 years of money market funds, bond funds, and other pooled accounts that specialize in interest-earning securities. While some instruments such as CDs and Treasury securities are easy to understand, corporate and municipal bonds are another matter. Investment in risk-bearing bonds requires a high amount of capital to achieve adequate diversification; investors may find it both easier and safer to use mutual funds as a way to invest.

In certain cases, preferred stock can be substituted for bonds, but because of tax considerations, they often are better suited to institutional investors. For more on preferred, read Chapter 9.

FIXED-INCOME OPTIONS

The vehicle an investor uses when investing in bonds and bond equivalents depends on the goal. If the goal is

- *Safety of capital:* The best investment is the direct purchase of a government security, a government-insured certificate of deposit at a financial institution, or shares in a money market fund. In these, the investor will always get the principal investment back, plus fixed- or variable-interest earnings.

- *To maximize high interest rates:* Bond mutual funds often capture the highest possible rate of return by the professional management of the fund. However, if there are abrupt changes in interest rates, the investor may find that the net asset value (NAV) per share, or the redemption price, is less than the initial investment. At least temporarily and on paper, the investor has lost money. The fund may recover its value as the markets adjust, but a bond fund offers no guaranteed return of principal plus interest.

DIVERSIFICATION
RULE NUMBER TWO

An investor needs to have a reasonably large number of shares in the portfolio—or, as Graham explained, "adequate but not excessive diversification."[8] Following the Crash of 1929 and during the Great Depression, Graham held portfolios with 75 or more stocks at a time. This was a large number of stocks, but Graham had a reason for buying so many:

> One of the mainstays of our operations was the rather undiscriminating purchase of common stocks at a price below their net-current-asset value, and later, sale, typically at prices to yield a profit of 20 percent or more per annum. Our portfolio often included more than 100 of such bargain issues at a given time; fully 90 percent of these returned satisfactory profits over the three and one-half decades.[9]

In other words, Graham was able to find many, many undervalued issues. Without paying excessive attention to quality, he bought a lot of different securities. The safety of the portfolio was ensured by spreading the risk over a large number of very cheap stocks. As time progressed, stocks of this type were increasingly difficult to find, forcing Graham to select stocks with greater care.

Occasionally today, companies—even well-established ones—can be purchased at such low prices that they warrant attention. There should be a special place for "Ben Graham Bargains" in a portfolio.

BENJAMIN GRAHAM BARGAINS

Oak Industries, an electronic controls and components company whose history goes back to the 1930s, became an overnight glamour stock in the early 1980s. The cable television industry, for which it made channel selection boxes and other equipment, suddenly took off and so did the manufacturer. But Oak wasn't as magical as its chief executive seemed to believe.

He celebrated increased sales by building and lavishly decorating a new headquarters building in Southern California, holding board meetings in Paris and indulging in other extravagances.

When the correction that so often occurs with technology stocks came, it was bloody. In 1984 the company lost $5.84 per share and Oak's tangible book value was a minus $3.62 per share. In 1983 the company suspended dividends that had been paid since 1934. The shares, which had traded in double-digit figures in the early 1980s, declined until in 1991 they traded at $1 per share, and occasionally even dipped below $1.

As it began its agonizing turnaround, the company went through several changes of management, moved to more modest headquarters, and sold off divisions simply to survive. By 1990 Oak Industries again began making money. By 1991 the tangible book value had risen to $1.02 per share, and earnings were 7 cents per share. The balance sheet and income statement numbers began to gradually climb, but the share price lingered around $1.

In 1993 Oak did a reverse 5-for-1 stock split to disabuse the company of its penny stock image. Then suddenly the stock's value was recognized. By 1995 the company was selling for $29 per share, which adjusted for the split would be about $5.80 per share. If an investor had purchased 100 shares in 1993 at $1 per share (a $100 investment), she would now hold 20 shares worth $580 dollars—an average growth rate of 240 percent per year.

But the good news just kept coming. By July 1995, Oak's share price had slipped a little to $26.50 per share, but *Barron's* included it in a list of stocks that fit Warren Buffett's criteria for acquisition. Among the requirements were companies with, among other things, a net income of 15 percent or more of sales and a 20 percent annual return on equity. Oak fit the bill. On the basis of its financial information, *Barron's* gave Oak a target price of $89.52. If shares rise that high, the investor who bought 100 shares for $1 in 1991 could sell them for $1790.40.

For the average investor following reasonably conservative guidelines, it is appropriate to hold as few as 5 stocks if they are of high quality or as many as 30 if they are of lesser quality. Anything more than that number becomes difficult to track, even with the use of a computer. While a computer can track price changes and provide easier access to research material, the investor still has to read all the material and understand the underlying companies.

The minimum of 5 stocks always is prudent because no more than 20 percent of an investor's portfolio should come from a single industry, but the maximum size of 30 different stocks in a portfolio is flexible. Limiting the number of shares in a portfolio is merely an attempt to make bookkeeping manageable and tracking of the portfolio easier. It is not dictated by a wish to improve returns. There is no maximum cutoff, as far as returns are concerned. "Returns are not diluted by an increased number of portfolio issues—so long as strict value criteria are followed," writes Charles Brandes.[10]

ONE WONDERFUL COMPANY

About the time a rule makes sense, someone suggests breaking it, if only in theory. Buffett has said that he wouldn't mind owning just one company, if it were a truly wonderful company. Since that "one perfect stock" is a rarity, Buffett advocates owning a manageable number of companies that you know and love for the right reasons. "Every new investment decision should be measured against what you already own. We measure every new investment against buying more Coca Cola. You should only buy if you like the new stock more than everything else that you own. The problem for most people is that it requires you to know what you own. If you own too many stocks, you can't possibly know them all. This is one of the most important investment lessons, and one of the easiest for an individual to follow, but often overlooked."[11]

INTERNATIONAL STOCKS

One of the most dramatic changes since Graham was alive and managing money is the explosion of international markets. In 1973, the year after Graham died, total global equity capitalization was $1.1 trillion. By 1994, it reached $14.1 trillion. During that same time period, the U.S. share of the world market shrank from 64 percent to 33 percent of the total. By investing only in the United States, an investor would miss:

- 10 of the 10 largest banking companies
- 10 of the 10 largest construction and housing companies
- 9 of the 10 largest public utility companies
- 8 of the 10 largest machinery companies
- 8 of the 10 largest electronics companies
- 7 of the 10 largest automobile companies
- 7 of the 10 largest chemical companies
- 7 of the 10 largest insurance companies.

Today investors seek out foreign markets in search of a wider range of opportunities to improve performance and diversification.

The young and smaller overseas markets have outperformed U.S. markets by a significant margin in recent years. Most Southeast Asian economies, for example, have grown at a minimum of 5 percent in each of the past 10 years, much better than in the United States. Even the mature securities markets in Germany, the United Kingdom, Hong Kong, France, Italy, Sweden, Norway, Japan, and Finland often outperform and seldom track U.S. markets. When bargains are scarce in this country, they may be plentiful elsewhere.[12]

Value investing principles are so fundamental that they apply equally to foreign investment markets. Many analysts insist that if Graham were alive today, he would be combing foreign markets for spectacular bargains. This may very well be true. Today's investors often are encouraged to have at least 10 percent, though no more than 20 percent, in overseas investments.

WATCH YOUR WALLET WHEN TRAVELING

On the other hand, foreign investment is fraught with dangers of its own, and Graham surely would be sounding his familiar warnings.

There are no fewer than 21 foreign stock exchanges with many hundreds of companies listed on each exchange. Information and corporate reporting on foreign-based investments may be difficult to come by and, in some cases, are of questionable quality. On top of that, investors are subjected to political risk, foreign currency exchange risk, inflation risk, and in some cases the risk that the chosen company will be nationalized. At the very least, foreign markets are highly volatile compared with the more mature U.S. stock markets.

THE BEST WAYS TO TRAVEL

Fortunately, there are several ways to diminish the risk and yet achieve diversification into the international marketplace. Invest in the following.

- *A closed-end mutual fund.* Closed-end funds are available that are global, regional, or country-specific in scope. Some of the oldest and most distinguished funds—The Japan Fund, among them—are closed-end country funds. Because a set number of shares are sold at the beginning of the fund, then investors buy and sell afterward like stocks, fund managers are less vulnerable to a sudden outflow of assets. This is a real threat to open-ended funds, especially when economic or political bad news floods a foreign market, causing investors to panic. It often is possible to find funds trading at up to a 20 percent discount from asset value. This discount creates an acceptable margin of safety. Again, these funds can be volatile in both price and return to investor.

- *A foreign company traded on a U.S. exchange via an American depository receipt (ADR).* Except for a few unusual cases, foreign companies listed on a U.S. exchange by ADR have agreed to meet that stock exchange's reporting rules. U.S. reporting regulations generally are more stringent than are rules abroad, so there is some assurance that financial figures are comparable to those reported by domestic corporations. ADRs actually are proxy or "stand-in" stocks held by a financial institution in the care of a shareholder. They are quoted and tracked, and dividends are paid in U.S. dollars. ADRs for approximately 1300 foreign companies are available in the United States. A good way to identify trustworthy ADR stocks is to scan the portfolios of the global, regional and country-specific funds.

- *A U.S. company with extensive overseas dealings.* Coca Cola, Walt Disney, International Business Machines, and Standard Oil Corporation are just a few of the companies that have extensive overseas suppliers, manufacturing facilities, and sales. They have been global for many years, have experience dealing in many different cultures, and know how to hedge currencies. At the same time, they have a documented financial record. Buffett says he does not buy foreign stocks, but participates internationally mainly through two investments, Coca Cola and Gillette.

THE TAX PRIVILEGE

Taxes play a major role in investing today, and though this subject deserves a book of its own, one rule is constant. Individual investors should place as much money as possible in tax-sheltered accounts such as individual retirement accounts or company 401-K plans. Often the contribution itself is exempt from taxes, and then earnings in the account compound tax-free, which speeds up growth.

It has long been a goal of the Republican Party to reduce capital gains taxes, but until that happens, investors can pay the lowest taxes on stock market earnings if securities are held at least a year. For gains on securities held less than a year, investors in a high tax bracket may pay a capital gains tax as high at 39.6 percent. For gains on securities held for a year or more, the maximum tax rate is 28 percent.

Beyond these basic guidelines, it's best to consult with a tax specialist with specific questions. At the same time, remember two old investor adages:

- Those who base their investment decisions on taxes sometimes end up with no taxes to worry about.
- Sometimes it's a privilege to pay taxes. It means you've made some money.

DOLLAR COST AVERAGING

Beginning investors often are advised to practice dollar cost averaging. Though Graham was not enamored of dollar cost averaging as a scientific way of buying stocks (after all, it implies that the investor doesn't know when a stock is undervalued), he believed it served a useful purpose for the typical investor. It gives investors discipline, he said. It keeps them from concentrating their buying at the wrong time—from responding to the emotional swings of the mercurial personality Graham called "Mr. Market."

Dollar cost averaging (also called the constant dollar plan) involves the investment of a fixed amount of dollars at set intervals. When applied to stocks, it forces the investor to buy more shares when the price is lower and fewer when the price is high. In this way the cost of shares purchased is always lower than the average share price for the investment period.

For the individual investor, an inexpensive (and easy) alternative to dollar cost averaging is to participate in the company's dividend reinvestment program.

REINVESTING DIVIDENDS

A dividend reinvestment plan (DRP) involves automatic reinvestment of dividends in more shares of the company's stock. An investor enrolls through the company after purchasing at least a minimum number of shares. Some companies absorb most of the brokerage fee, or charge a relatively small transaction fee. The share price is based on an average cost of the shares purchased by the company for the plan. Of course not all stocks pay dividends, and not all companies with dividends offer this service to shareholders.

Certainly a value investor should not use dollar cost averaging *or* participate in a DRP if a stock is overvalued. When such a stock reaches overvalue, the investor must decide whether to hold the stock for its dividend or to sell and reinvest in an alternative security.

PATIENCE

Too often an investor buys a stock, and then in the first 2 to 3 months, checks the price daily in the newspaper. If the stock has slipped, or even sticks right where it was when he bought it, the investor feels deflated. He's bought a dud. But not necessarily, said Graham:

Every investor should be prepared financially and psycho-logically for the possibility of poor short-term results. For example, in the 1973–74 decline the investor would have lost money on paper, but if he'd held on and stuck with the approach, he would have recouped in 1975–1976 and gotten his 15 percent average return for the five-year period.[13]

At Nicholas-Applegate, a San Diego investment firm, company pol-icy is to select undervalue securities, and to stay fully invested in them, because fund managers believe it is impossible to tell exactly when an undervalued issue will begin its share price ascent. Once the stock price starts to move upward, it can move very quickly. As Graham so often reminded investors, it is nearly impossible to predict the bottom or top of either an individual stock or the market as a whole. Nicholas-Applegate managers feel they have the best chance of capturing maxi-mum price appreciation by buying promising stocks and waiting patiently.

WHEN TO SELL

Many value investors buy with the intention of holding a stock as long as possible. If a company keeps on growing, why diminish a rate of return by paying broker fees and taxes? As pointed out earlier in the book, some original investors in Geico still own the stock, or have passed the stock along to subsequent generations of heirs. In 1993 Graham's grandson sold the shares of Geico he inherited to finance a degree in medicine. Geico went public in July of 1948.

"My favorite holding time is forever," says Warren Buffett.[14]

Yet value investors do sell. Buffett admits that sometimes he has to sell a stock he likes to buy another stock he likes better. Graham him-self regularly sold stocks that had either

- Appreciated 50 percent in value or
- Reached some other target price

Graham said any new stock should have the potential of upgrading the portfolio performance:

As an arbitrary rule, we might say that there should be good reason to believe that by making the exchange the investor would be getting at least 50 percent more for his money.[15]

PRUNING FOR BETTER PERFORMANCE

Money manager and former Graham employee Walter Schloss offers this observation: "A stock well-bought is half sold." By this Schloss means that, on the basis of net asset value, P/E ratio, and other factors, the investor has a fairly clear picture of what the stock's price should be. Unless there is some convincing change in the fundamentals, the stock can be sold when it rises significantly above the target price.[16]

It can take a stock as many as 3 to 5 years to move from undervalue to overvalue. Occasionally circumstances make it clear that the stock will not achieve an investment goal (when some fundamental factor is drastically changed), and in that case the stock should be sold at once.

Exceptional stocks can be held much longer than the typical holding period, however, because their growth potential continues to be strong for many years. Their intrinsic value, or future worth to an owner, continues to pace ahead of their market price. These stocks are the foundation of a virtually permanent portfolio.

Charles Dow advocated a similar strategy: "Cut your losses short, but let your profits run," he said. Unfortunately, he also noted, most investors do just the opposite.[17]

CONCLUSION

When investors lose money, it is generally because they flit too quickly from one type of investment to another. They consistently buy into an investment when it is "hot" or selling at its peak price, and sell when investment fervor has fled and the price has collapsed. The antidote for that self-destructive form of investing is to have a clear idea of what your portfolio should look like and to stick to that concept.

The portfolio should be purchased when good-quality securities are available at an advantageous price. Quality is the key to earning—and holding on to—high returns. "It's far better to own a significant portion of the Hope diamond than 100 percent of a rhinestone," Buffett tells us.[18]

IN THE MEANTIME, REMEMBER

- Set reasonable goals. A 12 to 15 percent average annual return is excellent.
- At all times keep at least 25 percent of your investment funds in bonds or the equivalent.
- At all times keep at least 25 percent of your investment funds in stocks.
- Never sell a stock without a solid reason to do so.
- Be patient.

Picking Stocks
of Value

If you are shopping for common stocks, choose them the way you would buy groceries, not the way you would buy perfume.[1]

BENJAMIN GRAHAM,
advice to the readers of *Mademoiselle* magazine, 1952

Graham's admonition to young ladies was sexist to be sure. Yet now, an era in which both women and men purchase groceries, cologne, *and* securities, the advice can be put in a new context. Graham's message is clear. All too often investors get caught up in the glamour of a stock. The company is written up in slick magazines; it is the topic at cocktail parties and on TV talk shows. It has charisma, and investors get captured by that. Forget the romance. Forget the fashion experts. Review the facts and apply simple but logical analysis.

BRINGING IT ALL TOGETHER

The time to integrate the evaluation of a company's safety, its growth potential, and your investment needs is just before you call your broker to place a buy order. While individual goals may vary, there is one objective all investors share. Very few of us *want* or *need* an underperforming stock. When choosing a stock, a value investor:

• Focuses on investment goals

• Uses balance sheet and income statement to get a range of intrinsic value

• Looks for a margin of safety

• Evaluates qualitative factors

A QUICK REVIEW

The first two points in the list above were covered in some detail in earlier chapters, but here are some reminders:

- Think total return. Investors can be rewarded by share price growth, by dividends, or by a combination of both, said Graham and Dodd:

> It is an almost unbelievable fact that Wall Street never asks, "How much is the business selling for?" Yet this should be the first question in considering a stock purchase. If a business man were offered a 5 percent interest in some concern for $10,000, his first mental process would be to multiply the asked price by 20 and thus establish a proposed value of $200,000 for the entire undertaking. The rest of his calculation would turn about the question whether or not the business was a "good buy" at $200,000.[2]

- "Price will tend to fluctuate around value," explains Roger Murray, a coauthor of the last edition of *Security Analysis*. Securities are chronically mispriced in relation to their intrinsic value, which gives investors the opportunity to buy low and sell high.[3]
- The range of intrinsic value lies somewhere between the asset value and a conservative multiple of earnings. For the most promising companies, this may be less than 20 times average earnings for the past 7 years, or less than 15 times earnings for the past 3 years. For companies under stress, look for a lower P/E.
- Watch out for debt overload, warned Graham and Dodd:

> Speculative capitalized enterprises, according to our definition, are marked by a relatively large amount of senior securities and a comparatively small issue of common stock.[4]

Keep those points in mind as, in the next few pages, we examine the margin of safety and the evaluation of qualitative factors in great depth, then review two different Graham approaches to buying stocks.

MARGIN OF SAFETY

Building a margin of safety starts with the establishment of a share price range for intrinsic value. Once an investor has a sense of what this future value to the owner might be, he looks for factors that establish a cushion against error. A *substantial excess of value* creates a comfortable margin of safety.

"Use an old Graham and Dodd guideline that you can't be that precise about a simple value," says Roger Murray. "Give yourself a band of 20 percent above or below, and say, 'that is the range of fair value.'"[5]

To achieve a margin of safety you must do one of the following:

- *Buy when the overall market is low and there are many undervalued issues.* (Market cycles are covered in Chapter 7).

- *Look for companies under temporary stress.*

There are numerous examples of companies that faced tragic and devastating news, causing the stock price to plunge. When the company is fundamentally sound, it often survives the crisis and the stock price eventually recovers. Such was the case with Exxon following the *Exxon Valdez* oil spill in Alaska in 1989; Louisiana Pacific in the 1990s after the company announced that it had been accused of violating the Clean Air Act and would face a stiff government fine; and perhaps the most cataclysmic of all, the Union Carbide accident in Bhopal, India.

In 1984 a Union Carbide plant leaked poisonous gas, killing thousands of people and maiming many, many more. Union Carbide's stock dove almost 27 percent over 10 trading days. Finally, it stabilized at around $5 per share. Yet 10 years after the disaster, the stock had rebounded nearly 400 percent, giving a yield of 700 percent if dividends were reinvested. Union Carbide's share price grew an average of 16 percent annually, outpacing the Standard & Poor's 500 index gain of 12 percent. In 1995 Union Carbide had a trading range between $25 and $43 per share.

- *Search for overlooked stocks even when the market is not particularly undervalued.* It is possible to find such stocks. Chrysler Corporation, described in Chapter 5, is one example. During a bear market, there are many bargains to be found. In a bull market, investors work harder for their gains, noted Graham and Dodd:

In either case, the "margin of safety" resides in the discount at which the stock is selling below its minimum intrinsic value, as measured by the analyst.[6]

TEN ATTRIBUTES OF AN UNDERVALUED STOCK

Professional investors have their favorite places to look for extra protection. An investor may accept different sources for that margin, depending on the circumstances and the investor's own zone of comfort. High asset value, strong cashflow, and dominant market position are among the influencing factors.

The first step is to examine the quantitative factors we've discussed earlier (net asset value, working capital, price-to-earnings ratio, debt-to-equity ratio, and so on). Graham made the following list of attributes of an undervalued stock. He noted that any company that meets 7 out of the 10 criteria is undervalued and has an adequate margin of safety.

Criteria 1 through 5 measure risk; 6 and 7 establish financial soundness; 8 through 10 show a history of stable earnings. Very few companies meet all 10 criteria.

1. An earnings-to-price yield (reverse of P/E ratio) that is double the AAA bond yield. If the AAA bond yield is 6 percent, the earnings yield should be 12 percent.

2. A price-to-earnings ratio that is four-tenths of the highest average P/E ratio achieved by the shares in the most recent 5 years.

3. A dividend yield of two-thirds the AAA bond yield. Stocks that lack either a dividend or current profits are automatically eliminated by this rule.

4. A stock price of two-thirds the tangible book value per share. The formula for tangible book value is given in Chapter 2.

5. A stock price that is two-thirds the net current asset value or the net quick liquidation value. This was the earliest investment technique used by Graham. These formulas are given in Chapter 3.

6. Total debt that is lower than tangible book value.

7. A current ratio of two or more. This is a measure of liquidity, or a company's ability to pay its debts from income. The current ratio formula is found in Chapter 3.

8. Total debt of no more than the net quick liquidation value.

9. Earnings that have doubled in the most recent 10 years.

10. Earnings that have declined no more than 5 percent in 2 of the past 10 years.[7]

These points are recommended only as guidelines. They should be given thoughtful attention, but should not be followed like a cookbook recipe. Some of the criteria in Graham's list are more important to certain investors than others. The three criteria an investor is willing to abandon depends on his or her investment goals.

• Investors who need income should pay special attention to criteria 1 through 7 and, in particular, insist that a stock adhere to criterion 3.

• Those who want a balance between safety and growth may ignore criterion 3 altogether, but focus on 1 through 5 and 9 and 10.

• Those who hope to achieve exceptional share price growth can ignore criterion 3; give lighter weighting to 4, 5 and 6; and give heavy weighting to 9 and 10.

By studying the list, investors can select those elements that best achieve their goals and compromise on those that do not.

Graham said that quantitative factors should rank ahead of qualitative factors when choosing a stock. However, qualitative factors can provide a comfortable margin of safety, and in unique cases can override the numbers when the arguments are convincing.

QUALITATIVE FACTORS

Warren Buffett of Berkshire Hathaway explains it this way: "The evaluation of securities and businesses for investment purposes has always involved a mixture of qualitative and quantitative factors. At one extreme, the analyst exclusively oriented to qualitative factors would say, 'Buy the right company (with the right prospects, inherent industry conditions, management, etc.) and the price will take care of itself.' One the other hand, the quantitative spokesman would say, 'Buy at the right price and the company (and stock) will take care of itself.' As so often is the pleasant result in the securities world, money can be made with either approach. And, of course, any analyst combines the two to some extent—his classification in either school would depend on the relative weight he assigns to the various factors and not to his consideration of one group of factors to the exclusion of the other group."[8]

Qualitative considerations may tip the scales when two stocks seem equally attractive, but when the investor can afford to buy only one, size, quality of the company and its products, the investor's special knowledge of an industry, and superior management all figure into the equation.

STABILITY OVER AGILITY

When it becomes difficult to choose between two stocks because their fundamentals are so similar, larger and more seasoned companies take precedence over unseasoned companies because of their stability, said Graham and Dodd. Established stocks usually hold value better in market swings because of an inertia that tends to work for them in falling markets but may prove to be a drag in a rising market:

> The untrained buyer fares best by purchasing goods of the highest reputation, even though he may pay a comparatively high price.[9]

SIZE NO HANDICAP

> As an offset to this we have the fact that the successful small company can multiply its value far more impressively than those which are already of enormous size.[10]

Nevertheless, Graham bought shares of both small and large companies and found that the growth of well-chosen large companies also can be very rapid.

It is a deeply and long-held belief among investors that the share prices of stocks of smaller companies tend to perform better than those of larger companies. Researchers now confirm that the small-cap advantage was a mistake, based on a misinterpretation of numbers. What the research actually shows is that companies that are deeply undervalued—and their total market value is relatively small for that reason—are the better performers. Despite the new evidence, writes investment columnist David Dreman, "I cannot pick up a business or financial publication that does not have someone saying that small stocks are the place to be today. Old canards die hard."[11]

BONUS POINTS FOR KNOWING THE INDUSTRY

Buffett advises investors to stay within their own circle of competence. "Our principles are valid when applied to technology stocks but we don't know how to do it," he told Berkshire Hathaway shareholders. "If we are going to lose your money, we want to be able to get up here next year and explain how we did it. I'm sure Bill Gates (of Microsoft Corp.) would apply the same principles. He understands technology the way I understand Coca Cola or Gillette. I'm sure he looks for a margin of safety. I'm sure he would approach it like he was owning a business and not just a stock. So our principles can work for any technology. We just aren't the ones to do it. If we can't find things within our circle of competence, we won't expand the circle. We'll wait."[12]

Though Buffett used Coca Cola and Gillette as companies he understands thoroughly, he also is exceptionally well versed in the insurance industry, which represents a substantial portion of Berkshire Hathaway's assets. His first lesson on how the insurance world works occurred when, as a graduate student, he took Geico on as a seminar project.

Investing in companies that you know well, says Charles Brandes, of Brandes Investment Partners, means "you won't give way to scare headlines that could influence you over the short term. Also, understanding the business acts as a spur and facilitates digging that may be necessary."[13]

THE MANAGEMENT CHECK

Management's contribution to making a stock more valuable tomorrow than it is today is a subject that arises time and time again. This we know. The most important thing investors want management to do is run a profitable company. Next, they want those profits to be utilized so as to enhance the shareholder's net worth, the company's net worth, or both.

"Buying back shares is the simplest and best way a company can reward its investors," explains former manager of the Fidelity's Magellen Fund Peter Lynch, but it's not the only way.[14] "The common alternatives to buying back shares are (1) raising the dividend, (2) developing new products, (3) starting new operations, and (4) making acquisitions," Lynch continued.[15]

The last three alternatives provide less of a guaranteed return to investors, but they are positive developments nonetheless.

THE BENJAMIN GRAHAM WAYS

During his lifetime Graham continually searched for even better ways to select stocks. He ran various tests on the absolute best criteria for identifying safe stocks that would deliver a high investment return. He searched for a method that was logical and simple, and one that delivered a satisfactory return over a long period, including market slumps.

Long after he had retired, the 80-year-old Graham put forth an advanced set of criteria which became the guiding principles for an investment fund he started with a friend, the Rae-Graham Fund. Those are included in his 10 criteria for an undervalued stock, listed earlier in this chapter. Though Graham's goal may have been simplicity, most investors find the 10 criteria somewhat technical. The different methods Graham presented in his book and other writings are, in fact, only variations of his fundamental principles. Research has shown that all provide relative safety and a return higher than that earned by the Dow Jones Industrial Average.

THE DEFENSIVE INVESTOR

A conservative investor can hardly go wrong by applying the "rules for the stock market component" Graham described in *The Intelligent Investor*, popularized in some of his magazine articles, and taught in his classes. The guidelines are about as simple as you can get.

An investor interested in low portfolio maintenance, low investment costs, and a high level of protection should consider the following seven requirements for a company:

- Adequate size ($100 million in annual sales, at least $50 million in assets)
- Sufficiently strong financial condition (a 2-to-1 current ratio)
- Continuous dividend payment for the past 20 years
- No earnings deficit for at least 10 years
- A minimum 33.3 percent earnings growth over the past 10 years
- A share price of no more than 1.5 times net asset value
- A share price of no more than 15 times average earnings for the past 3 years[16]

This strategy eliminates virtually every so-called growth stock, but investors will benefit from stability and growth over long periods of time. Companies that end up in this "buy and hold" portfolio usually don't have steep share price climbs in bull markets, but their growth is dependable. They decline less when the market falls. As a result, like the tortoise of legend, they often arrive ahead of the hare.

AN AGGRESSIVELY MANAGED PORTFOLIO

In a speech he made in the early 1970s, Graham outlined an adaptation of some of his earlier investment practices to modern markets. As explained previously, much of his initial success was based on finding extremely cheap stocks, buying many undervalued stocks, and expecting the fast-track stocks to make up for those that fell by the wayside:

Our techniques themselves must seem too simple to be convincing. They involve no forecasts of the economy or of the stock market, and no selectivity among industries and individual companies. The sole reliance is placed on a single criterion of price attractiveness, applied indiscriminately on a group basis.[17]

Such a strategy depends on being able to find extremely inexpensive issues—an approach that has become increasingly difficult since the end of World War II. In his 1973 modification of his earlier techniques, Graham showed that investors who are willing to put time and effort into research, tracking, and portfolio management could still achieve a higher return by buying extremely cheap stocks.

THE FINELY TUNED PORTFOLIO

In an approach presented in 1975, Graham suggested following these portfolio management rules:

- Build a portfolio of approximately 30 issues of stocks chosen at random from stocks that meet the standards below.
- Set a target profit for each issue of 50 percent above cost, to be attained within 2 years.
- All issues that don't appreciate at least 50 percent in 2 years should be sold at their market price at the end of 2 years.

For this portfolio, Graham recommended that investors buy stocks that meet the following standards:

- An attractive P/E ratio (or an earnings-to-price ratio—opposite of P/E) of twice the last 12 months' yield on Moody's AAA bonds, but never less than 10
- An attractive dividend yield (in most markets, a range of 3 to 6 percent)
- A price below book value (if you can find them, those stocks at about two-thirds of book are preferred)
- A price well below the previous high (perhaps one-half the market high of the past 2 years)
- An attractive price in relation to past earnings growth (a P/E lower than the 7- to 10-year average P/E)

Graham ran tests using various price-to-earnings ratios and book values, and whatever tinkering he did, the portfolio generated high returns. (Though he recommended applying the dividend and earnings growth criteria, the tests that gave the following results did not include them because he had insufficient information.) Graham said:

By any of our simple methods [variations on P/E and book values] the investor could have averaged 5 percent to 15 percent greater than in a typical NYSE random portfolio.[18]

The very best results came from emphasizing a low P/E ratio, as described above. The real-life story of Pinnacle West Capital shows how a potential stock purchase might hold up under the type of scrutiny described in this and previous chapters. Pinnacle West is an example of one stock that didn't quite make the grade.

A VALUE-BASED REVIEW OF PINNACLE WEST CAPITAL

Pinnacle West Capital Corp., an Arizona public utility, was recommended in 1995 by several investment newsletters as an excellent buy. Pinnacle West has a real estate development component, but 98 percent of its revenues come from its public utility subsidiary, Arizona Public Power. In the early 1980s Pinnacle West tried to diversify into banking and real estate. The financial services venture turned out badly, and the company finally got out of the business. Since then Pinnacle West has been on the rebound. Arizona Public Power, incidentally, operates a nuclear power station, which adds an element of risk for electric utility companies. Let's start the evaluation by running Pinnacle West's numbers through Graham's formula for intrinsic value.

$$E(2r + 8.5) \times 4.4 / Y$$

Using 1995 figures for Pinnacle West Capital Corp., the company's intrinsic value would be calculated as follows:

E (earnings per share) = \$2

r (expected earnings growth rate) = 5.27 % (calculated from *Value Line* estimated numbers)

Y (current yield on AAA corporate bonds) = 7.37 %

$$\$2 \ (2 \times 5.27 + 8.5) \times 4.4 / 7.37 = \$22.73$$

At the time of the calculation Pinnacle West was trading for around \$25 per share, a price just

(Pinnacle West Capital con't) above its estimated intrinsic value.

As a second check on whether Pinnacle West should be considered for purchase, let's see how the share price stacks up against other measures of value. Here are some additional facts:

- *Book Value.* The shares had a book value of $21.40, so they were trading near, but nevertheless above book value.

- *Debt.* Debt was 53 percent of equity—on the high side, but not frighteningly high.

- *P/E ratio.* The price-to-earnings ratio was 11, within Graham's range of value.

- *Earnings trend.* Average earnings between 1984 and 1994 were $1.99, the exact amount of the company's last reported annual earnings in 1994. For 1995 earnings were expected to be $2, and for 1996 they were estimated at $2.20. Overall, earnings were a mixed bag. They were strong from 1984 to 1987, at which time they began to slip. There was a $3.90 per share earnings deficit in 1991, and again earnings began to rise, but not at a remarkable speed.

- *Share price standard.* At $25 per share, the stock was trading near its high for the past 2 years.

- *Dividend history and yield.* Dividends were suspended in 1991, 1992, and 1993, then restored in 1993. Both the dividend yield and the payout are low compared with other public utilities.

For Graham's defensive investor, this company would be ruled out, based on its dividend record, its weak earnings deficit, and its inadequate per share earnings growth. The stock would be eliminated for the more aggressive investor for three reasons. Its price is too high in relation to past prices; its high price is more than two-thirds the book value, and its dividend yield is low.

The stock may have been appropriate for purchase if its record were stronger and its share price had not moved out of range. During the time of this report, management was reducing debt and plowing back a substantial portion of profits to retained earnings. The company may eventually become a more attractive buy. But at the time of this analysis there were more promising stocks to choose from.

Value Line confirms this evaluation in a report written May 6, 1995. "Overall, progress is evident across the financial front. But the stock is not recommended for conservative investors at this time."[19]

DIGGING UP UNDERVALUED STOCKS

As emphasized earlier, undervalued stocks can be purchased either by choosing among an abundance of low-priced stocks when the market is floundering or by searching out overlooked stocks when share prices in general are not depressed. Often, a temporary bargain price occurs when a company is hit with a barrage of bad news. In many such circumstances investors overreact to initial negative news and a fundamentally sound stock is undervalued—at least until the hysteria subsides.

Additionally, when markets are strong investors should keep a bargain hunter's eye on industries that, for some reason or another, swim against the tide. From 1990 to 1995, financial service, medical, and utility stocks all were on the investor's black list. Yet common sense tells us that there will continue to be banks, pharmaceuticals manufacturers, hospitals, and electric power companies. When the clouds over these industries clear, stock prices of the companies will rise.

Companies with deeply discounted stocks are often found in geographical areas that are awash in negativity. Somehow people think bad news will go on forever. Texas, Colorado, and Massachusetts all took their turn in the economic dumpster during the last two decades. Some people moved away from these states in search of jobs, but the areas did not become deserted nor did all economic activity cease. Yet many companies based in these regions were battered by pessimism.

California recently underwent a similar episode when the aerospace industry suffered from federal government cuts. Yet California is the seventh largest economy in the world, and it's a good bet that there will continue to be a California. While gloom and doomers dominated the news, value investors trolled California for undervalued banks, utilities, oil companies, and real estate operations.

FINDING THE INFORMATION YOU NEED

The traditional way—and still the easiest—to find investment bargains is by keeping up with financial news and using the traditional stock information services. Scour *The Wall Street Journal* each day for companies hitting new lows in the stock price columns. If you can check prices only periodically, subscribe to *Barron's*, a weekly publication. Some daily newspapers publish a weekly summary of stock market prices each Sunday.

When you read the financial press, you'll be bombarded with pitches for sophisticated sources of investment information. When considering such services, measure the quality of the information and its timeliness versus the cost.

Professional investors may find such services as Ford Investor Services or Dow Jones Telerate to be worth the price. However, these intricate and sometimes specially tailored sources of information often cost more than an individual investor will earn on a portfolio each year. For more information on computerized sources, turn to Chapter 10.

OFF TO THE LIBRARY

Even with the avalanche of information available electronically, many investors still trek to the library to review the traditional sources of information—Value Line and Standard & Poor's stock reports. Warren Buffett uses Value Line, though he complains that the 10 years of information presented is not sufficient. He, according to lore, saves old copies so that he can search back further for information.

In addition to reports on the companies themselves, Standard & Poor's and Value Line supply worthwhile research and screens of the market in general. Investors will find a compendium of stock market averages, median P/E ratios for the market, and other compilations. Value Line, for example, scans market data for lists of high-yielding securities, cash-generating companies, stocks trading below book value, stocks with low P/E ratios, companies with high return on capital, and so forth. An investor can save many hours of work by scanning these lists for stock purchase ideas.

For more information on financial publications, check the suggested reading list at the back of this book.

COMPANY A VERSUS COMPANY B

It can be a helpful exercise to compare companies within an industry to one another. Why buy one company when a competitor may be better? Why buy Merck if Bristol-Myers Squibb will bring a higher return? But comparisons also can be distracting.

When comparing one stock with another, Benjamin Graham cautioned, don't get carried away deciding whether Company A is superior to Company B as an investment, without deciding in the first place whether A is a desirable investment in its own right. It's possible that you should own neither A stock nor B stock. Or you may decide to own both.

BUYING A STOCK IS ONLY THE BEGINNING

In the chapters ahead we'll address a range of other topics that can help an investor refine and manage a portfolio better. Once you purchase a stock you become an owner, and, Graham and Dodd pointed out, there are certain responsibilities attendant on ownership. You must vote on corporate proposals, pay taxes on dividends, monitor performance, and decide whether to sell or stay:

> The choice of a common stock is a single act; its ownership is a continuing process. Certainly there is just as much reason to exercise care and judgment in *being* as in *becoming* a stockholder.[20]

CONCLUSION

In a lecture Graham gave at the New York Institute of Finance in 1947, he delivered a "sound bite" for investment advisers:

> Investors do not make mistakes, or bad mistakes, in buying good stocks at fair prices. They make their serious mistakes by buying poor stocks, particularly the ones that are pushed for various reasons, and sometimes—in fact, very frequently—they make mistakes by buying good stocks in the upper reaches of bull markets.[21]

With the lessons learned thus far, perhaps investors can avoid paying too much for a stock, regardless of when it is acquired. Once the stock has been purchased the value investor must develop the virtue of patience. It may take many months before the value of a business becomes recognized—sometimes as long as 3 to 5 years. "The goal of the value investor is not a sudden run-up and quick cash out," explains Charles Brandes, "but finding an outstanding business at a sensible price, or a mediocre business at a bargain price."[22]

Finally, keep in mind that no investor makes correct choices 100 percent of the time. Even Warren Buffett bought U.S. Air, which fell from an airline with a future to a struggling airline and eventually suspended payment of preferred stock dividends. (To be fair, U.S. Air paid high dividends to Berkshire Hathaway for several years before it suspended. The investment wasn't a total loss.)

IN THE MEANTIME, REMEMBER

- Seek a margin of safety.

> We obtain this protection by insisting upon margins of safety, or values well in excess of the price paid. The underlying idea is that even if the security turns out to be less attractive than it appeared, the commitment might still prove a satisfactory one.[23]

- Seek quality measured by a company's history, its key numbers, and its management.
- Small or new investors should avoid buying stocks in new or virtually new ventures, trading in the market, and purchasing so-called growth stocks, especially at the height of a buying fever.
- Follow Graham and Dodd's admonition to think for yourself:

> The public buys issues that are sold to it, and the sales effort is put forward to benefit the seller and not the buyer.[24]

7

Thriving in Every Market

In almost every other walk of life, people buy more at lower prices; in the stock and bond market they seem to buy more at higher prices.[1]

JAMES GRANT

The October 1987 crash was a learning lab for all serious investors. As a result, investors came to understand that markets are never cured of their propensity to overheat and then to overcorrect. Markets may be continually in search of intrinsic value, but they do it the way a hunting dog searches for a scent. They rush madly back and forth across the clue, sniffing everywhere. The process can appear quite frenetic, even when the dog is on the track.

"Disregarding for the moment whether the prevailing level of stock prices on January 1, 1987, was logical, we are certain that the *value* of American industry in the aggregate had not increased by 44 percent as of August 25. Similarly, it is highly unlikely that the *value* of American industry declined by 23 percent on a single day, October 19," wrote William Ruane and Richard Cunniff in the Sequoia Fund 1987 third-quarter report.[2]

When a stock is undervalued, the stage is set for reversal. On that April 1995 day when Kirk Kerkorian and Lee Iacocca made a takeover move on Chrysler, did the actual value of the stock rocket from $39 per share to $55 per share overnight? Probably not. By most analytical standards, with a price-to-earnings ratio of 4, Chrysler was undervalued at $39. The takeover bid alerted investors to Chrysler's situation, and at the beginning of September 1995, nearly 4 months afterward, the shares were still trading at around $55; even then the P/E was only 8.

Such is the scatterbrained behavior of someone Benjamin Graham called "Mr. Market."

MR. MARKET

Mr. Market is an emotional wreck! His hair is unkempt. His nails are chewed to the quick. He endlessly taps his fingers on the desktop. He rushes from one crisis to the next, and if he has to sit for any length of time, his knee twitches compulsively. How does he keep his job on Wall Street? He *is* Wall Street.

Think of Mr. Market as a confused and changeable business partner, Graham told his students. Warren Buffett described Mr. Market's business tactics. "Even though the business that the two of you own may have economic characteristics that are stable," wrote Buffett, "Mr. Market's quotations will be anything but. For, sad to say, the poor fellow has incurable emotional problems."[3]

Mr. Market is compulsive. He shows up every day and makes an offer for your part of the business. If you ignore him he is neither offended nor deterred. He will be there again the next day, and the next, and the next.

Also manic depressive, Mr. Market sometimes becomes euphoric. During these spells he can see only blue skies ahead and endless climbing profits. During those times he rushes in and offers an unrealistically high price for your shares. At the slightest negative news, Mr. Market's spirits dive. His price then is ridiculously low.

But pay no attention to the mood swings. "Mr. Market is there to serve you, not to guide you," Buffet explained.[4]

If his offer meets your needs as an investor, you can accept it. If it does not, you may ignore it. If you take advantage of him, Mr. Market never remembers. Crazy as he is, Mr. Market is a convenient business partner.

To say that a value investor does not "play the market" is not to say that market cycles don't exist and that they do not play an important role in the work of investing. One needs only to examine a chart of the movement of the Dow Jones Industrial Average over a long period of time—10, 20 years or more—to see that there are wavelike advances and retreats in aggregate stock prices. Value investors realize that they cannot predict how low or how high a market indicator will move, or when a reversal will come. Market ebbs and flows are, admits Graham, an essential part of successful investing.

SUITABLE SECURITIES AT SUITABLE PRICES

The investor's primary interest lies in acquiring and holding suitable securities at suitable prices. Market movements are important to him in a practical sense, because they alternately create low price levels at which he would be wise to buy and high price levels at which he certainly should refrain from buying and probably would be wise to sell.[5]

Though market conditions are easy to see in hindsight; they are, according to *Security Analysis*, almost impossible to predict in the near or distant future:

In a sense, the market and the future present the same kind of difficulties. Neither can be predicted or controlled by the analyst, yet his success is largely dependent on both of them.[6]

PAYING RESPECT TO THE MARKET

Though timing purchases and sales of stocks to coincide with market lows and highs often proves fruitless, value investors share two assumptions with the market timer:

• The market is frequently out of alignment with true value.
• There is a tendency for the market to correct itself.

Furthermore, both market timers and value investors intuitively and empirically know that market movements and fundamental value are related. Somehow, the price of a company eventually rises (and sometimes crashes) to realign with its actual value. Changing conditions, new information, or perhaps the awakening of investors to existing circumstances draws the market as surely as the moon draws the sea.

PEAKS, MEADOWS, AND VALLEYS

What makes trends so difficult to spot in the short run is that, when charted, stock markets aren't shaped like Mt. Fuji—a steady rise to a level top, where there's a nice flat place that gives the investor an opportunity to take in the view and take profits before starting the trip back down. Rather the markets resemble the Sierra Nevada mountains—zigzagging up and down, with each peak getting higher than the last until you reach Mt. Whitney's summit. Markets are like mountains in another way. The trip down from the summit always seems faster and scarier than the climb. Unlike mountains, though, financial markets are being created as you go.

MARKET ANALYSIS

Investors are continually bombarded with market analyses, all of which fall into one of two categories:

- The first approach is backward looking. It constitutes "chart reading" of past behavior.
- The second is forward looking. It anticipates interest rate changes, industry cycles, business and political conditions that might impact corporate earnings or investor attitude.

Neither, according to Graham and Dodd, is a science. The past performance of the economy, of the market, or of an individual issue is no guarantee of future performance. Forward looking analysis introduces multiple unknown variables—any of which could be forecasted imperfectly.

Chart reading invariably evolves from the studies and writing of Charles H. Dow, of Dow Jones fame, a respected investment journalist who covered Wall Street in the late nineteenth century and the first few years of the twentieth century. Graham had little patience with so-called Dow theorists. Their risks were unnecessarily high, he believed.

Trading on market movements seems easier and may be more profitable in the short run, but it is more difficult for market traders to accumulate long-run profits and hold on to gains:

> In market analysis there are no margins of safety; you are either right or wrong, and if you are wrong, you lose money.[7]

Yet while Graham rejected the theories that Dow's followers developed after his death, Graham may very well have respected Dow's own teachings. Both men took a conservative approach to investments. Both Graham and Dow viewed the stock market as a risky place where investors can make money as long as they keep their heads about them.

GRAHAM VERSUS DOW

Benjamin Graham often denounced the use of the Dow theory, a market timing method that relies on specific market configurations to send buy and sell signals. These signals, say Dow theory practitioners, are confirmed, when one average follows the behavior of another.

While the method has been successful in some market stretches, it has not proved consistent over the long haul, Graham claimed. For the 30-year period between 1938 and 1968, for example, Graham's research showed that Dow theory investors would have done considerably better by simply buying and holding the DJIA.[8]

Despite Dow's fascination with market movements, he and Graham had much in common. They shared the belief that changes in intrinsic value motivate the markets. "To know values is to comprehend the meaning of movements in the market," Dow wrote.[9]

Dow, a reserved Connecticut Yankee by birth and nature, was the founder and first editor of *The Wall Street Journal*. Considering his short tenure as the newspaper's editor and stock market columnist—Dow launched the paper in 1889 but died in 1902—his influence on investment ideology has been vast.

(Graham Versus Dow con't)

Dow's own writings contain so many cautious caveats that they very nearly repudiate the elaborate investment system developed by his followers after his death. Dow insisted not only that prices depend on values, but that values are determined by earnings. While he argued that no chart could foretell a company's true future prospects, he did believe that a shrewd "speculator" could benefit from buying and selling in cadence with the market.

Dow noted that the securities market, like every other thing in nature, behaves rhythmically. The stock market, he observed, displayed a pattern of rhythms within rhythms. The market has its daily swings. The daily movements occur within longer oscillations with an average periodicity of 30 to 40 days. The 30- to 40-day waves merge into longer bull or bear trends that can last for as long as 4 to 6 years.

"Nothing is more certain than that the market has three well-defined movements which fit into each other," Dow wrote.[10] Within that structure an individual stock can have cycles of its own, sometimes moving with the market and sometimes not. In the case of either the market or of a specific security, all the future is not revealed in charts.

"In dealing with the stock market there is no way of telling when the top of an advance or the bottom of a decline has been reached until some time after such top or bottom has been made," wrote Dow in a 1902 column. "Sometimes people are able to guess when prices are at the top or at the bottom, but such guesses are of their nature not of particular value, and it is a proverb in Wall Street, that only a foolish speculator hopes to buy stocks at the lowest and sell them at the highest. The speculator with experience knows that no one can do this with certainty or regularity."[11]

So Mr. Graham and Mr. Dow aren't in such different orbits after all.

TIMING VERSUS PRICING

Since market cycles obviously do exist, wise value investors will make the best of them. There are two possible ways of taking advantage of the swings, Graham says:

- Timing
- Pricing

Research tends to confirm Graham's belief that market timing, or anticipating the swings in advance, simply does not hold up. A 1995 study of market timing newsletter recommendations found that 75 percent did not do as well as a basic buy-and-hold strategy based on Standard & Poor's 500 stock index. In cases where a newsletter beat the market for 2 years in a row, the newsletter had a less than 50 percent chance of doing so for a third year.[12]

Since timing is well-nigh impossible, Graham suggested the pricing approach. By buying and selling on the basis of price, an investor will not have bought or sold in anticipation of a bull or bear market, but only after the fact. The investor buys after she knows that prices have declined and securities are undervalued. She sells when a bull market has pushed prices beyond the intrinsic value of the stock or bond.

By selling overvalued securities at the market's zenith and resolutely holding cash, the investor will have the reserve funds to buy bargain issues when the market is at its nadir. Though market swings cannot be reliably and consistently predicted, they can be exploited once they occur.

BELIEVING A BULL MARKET

When markets are rapidly rising, value investing invariably falls out of favor with the investing public. Benjamin Graham's son, who owns the royalty rights for *Security Analysis* and *The Intelligent Investor*, says his father's books generally sell poorly when the market is roaring. At that time almost all investors feel they have the ability to pick a winning stock. In an upward racing market, value stocks appear dull and stodgy as the more speculative issues rush toward new market highs. But come the correction, it all looks different. Stable value stocks seem like trusted friends, and the sale of Graham's books picks up accordingly.

Most bull markets have well-defined characteristics. These include:

- Price levels are historically high.
- Price-to-earnings ratios are high.
- Dividend yields are low compared with bond yields (or compared with a stock's particular dividend yield pattern).
- Margin buying becomes excessive as investors are driven to borrow to buy more of the high-priced stocks that look attractive to them.

- There is a swarm of new stock offerings, especially initial public offerings (IPOs) of questionable quality. This bull market is what investment bankers and stock promoters call the "window of opportunity." Because IPOs so often occur when Wall Street is primed to pay top dollar, seasoned investors joke that IPO stands for "it's probably overpriced."

THE PAUSE AT THE TOP OF THE ROLLER COASTER

There is only one strategy that works for value investors when the market is high—patience. The investor can do one of two things, both of which require steady nerves.

- Sell all stocks in a portfolio, take profits, and wait for the market to decline. At that time, many good values will present themselves. This may sound easy, but it pains many investors to sell a stock when its price is still rising.
- Stick with those stocks in the portfolio that have long-term potential. Sell only those that are clearly overvalued, and once more wait for the market to decline. At this time, value stocks may be appreciating at slow pace compared with the frisky growth stocks, but not always.

But come the correction, be it sudden or slow, the well-chosen value stocks have a better chance of holding their price.

The portfolio of one value investor shows what can happen when markets stumble off a cliff. In early September 1987, Walter Schloss's portfolio was up 53 percent. The market as a whole had risen 42 percent, after a DJIA peak of 2722.42. Then in October the market fell off the mountain and the Dow lost 504 points in a single day. The market struggled back and Schloss finished 1987 with a 26 percent gain, while the overall market made only a 5 percent advance. Schloss followed one of the first rules of investing—don't lose money. Making up for lost ground puts an investor at a serious disadvantage when calculating long-term average annual returns.

Schloss is an experienced investor, and not all value investors will do as well in a rising market. It takes practice. "At a guess I'd say that [the value investor] should do a good 20 percent better than the market over a long period—although not during the most dynamic period of a bull market—if he is rigorous about applying the method," says author John Train.[13]

As for the hot stocks, when they take a hard hit the investor is cornered. If the stock is sold, the loss becomes permanent. The lost money cannot grow. If the investor hangs on to the deflated stock, the long trail back to the original purchase price will deeply erode the overall return.

MAKING FRIENDS WITH A BEAR

When corrections come quickly, the question always arises: Is this a repeat of 1929? Will brokers be jumping out of windows? Is this the start of another Great Depression? Certainly Graham knew about such experiences. Though he realized the 1929 stock market was on dangerously high ground, he'd chosen his investments carefully and hedged his accounts. Graham believed he'd protected his accounts, yet he'd failed to fully execute all his hedges and he'd overused margin. His accounts were badly damaged by the crash. Nevertheless he hung in, rebuilt his portfolio, and soon afterward triggered a market recovery by telling the world that the time to resume buying had arrived.

BARGAINS AT THE BOTTOM

In 1932 Graham was 38 years old and had already made and lost millions of dollars. To survive the Great Depression he taught at several universities, testified as an expert witness in securities cases, wrote freelance pieces for the financial press, and with his partner, Jerome Newman, bought and liquidated defunct companies.

In June 1942, *Forbes* published the first in a series of articles written by Graham alerting investors that the shares of many companies were selling at prices below the value of the actual cash held in the company vaults. The series was called "Is American Business Worth More Dead Than Alive?"

Graham pointed out that 30 percent of the companies listed on the NYSE were selling at less than their net working capital, with some going for less than their cash assets. In other words, if an investor bought all the shares of a company, then sold off its assets, he would reap considerable profits. That series of articles was widely read. It gave dispirited investors the courage to return to the stock market and spurred a long, sustained recovery.[14]

Graham's wisdom inspired investors again in 1974, when the stock market was in a deep depression. He addressed the annual meeting of the Institute of Chartered Financial Analysts (which he helped found), the predecessor to the Association for Investment Management and Research (AIMR). In a speech entitled "A Renaissance of Value," Graham pointed out that once more, stocks were selling at deep discounts to their intrinsic value. "How long will such 'fire-sale stocks' continue to be given away?" he asked. Graham encouraged the investment managers to buy as many bargain issues as possible while prices were low. The Dow, at the time, had receded to 600.[15]

Again, Graham sounded the wake-up call that led to a market revival. By 1976 the DJIA topped 900.

SIGNS AT THE BOTTOM

The bottom—or near enough the bottom—of a market cycle theoretically should be easier to call than the top or near top. The evidence is found in the corporate balance sheets, income statements, P/E ratios, dividend yields, and other quantitative measures. It is likewise reflected in low ratios for the market as a whole. The quantitative factors speak for themselves.

The dividend yield on the Dow Jones Industrial Average, for example, usually cycles between a high yield of 6 percent at the market's bottom and a low yield of 3 percent at the top. The Dow's average dividend yield sometimes stretches beyond these boundaries, but historically this is a trustworthy parameter of undervalue and overvalue.

BUYING TIME

When the market hits its low, true value investors feel that harvest time has arrived. "The most beneficial time to be a value investor is when the market is falling." says investment manager Seth Klarman.[16] There are plenty of companies ripe for the picking. In the summer of 1973, when the stock market had plunged 20 percent in value in less than 2 months, Warren Buffett told a friend, "You know, some days I get up and I want to tap dance."

Unfortunately, this is the time when investors are feeling most beat up by the markets. Fear and negative thinking prevail, and anyone who has faced down a bear knows how paralyzing fear can be. This, at the depths of a bear market, is the time to buy as many stocks as are affordable. "Value bargains aren't found in strong markets," writes money manager Charles Brandes. "A good rule is to examine stock markets that have reacted adversely for a year or so."[17]

IF YOU ABSOLUTELY MUST PLAY THE HORSES

Though Ben Graham in no way recommended trying it, he did say that there is a way to combine market timing and value investing principles. This method was originally developed by Roger Babson, a contemporary of Graham's who provided financial services and investment counsel. However, Graham noted, the method makes heavy demands on human fortitude, and it can keep an investor out of long stretches of a booming market. It sounds simple. Yet for those who realize how difficult it is to follow, this strategy can diminish the risk of trading on market movements.

Here is the way it works:

1. Select a diversified list of common stocks. (The investor can even create an index fund by buying the DJIA, or better yet, deciding which stocks are undervalued in the DJIA and buying only those.)

2. Determine a normal value for each stock (choose any multiplier of earnings that seems appropriate, using 7- to 10-year average earnings).

3. Buy the stocks when shares can be bought at a substantial discount—say, two-thirds of what the investor has established as normal value. As an alternative to buying at one target price, the investor can

(If You Must Play the Horses con't) start buying as the stock declines, beginning at 80 percent of normal value.

4. Sell the stocks when the price has risen substantially above normal value—say, 20 percent to 50 percent higher.

The investor thus would buy in a market decline and sell in a rising market.[18]

Undervalued stocks quite often lie dormant for months—many months—on end. The only way to anticipate and catch the surge is to identify the undervalued situation, then take a position, and wait, Graham said:

> Buying a neglected and therefore undervalued issue for profit generally proves a protracted and patience-trying experience.[19]

CONCLUSION

It is essential for a value investor to understand the nature and the tendencies of the market. Steady nerves are the only defense against the euphoria that spreads as the market rises and the depressive reaction as the market corrects. Mr. Market's mood is communicable to the uninoculated:

> The market is not a *weighing machine* on which the value of each issue is recorded by an exact and impersonal mechanism, in accordance with its specific qualities. Rather should we say that the market is a *voting machine*, whereon countless individuals register choices which are the product partly of reason and partly of emotion.[20]

RELATIONSHIP OF INTRINSIC VALUE FACTORS TO MARKET PRICE

A. Speculative

1. Market factors
   - a. Technical
   - b. Manipulative
   - c. Psychological

2. Future value factors
   - a. Management and reputation
   - b. Competitive conditions and prospects
   - c. Possible and probable changes in volume, price, and costs

B. Investment

3. Intrinsic value factors
   - a. Earnings
   - b. Dividends
   - c. Assets
   - d. Capital structure
   - e. Terms of the issue
   - f. Others

Attitude of public →Bids and →Market
toward the issue   Offers   Price

Source: Security Analysis (New York: McGraw-Hill, 1940), p. 27.

IN THE MEANTIME, REMEMBER

- Understand the market's reason for being. "It is important that an issue be readily saleable, it is still more important that it command a satisfactory price," said Graham.[21]

- Just because a stock seems cheap or dear doesn't mean that it should be bought or sold. "Value in relation to price, not price alone, must determine your investment decisions," advises Klarman.[22]

- Though investors cannot predict market conditions, they can take advantage of conditions once they are recognized.

- It's not a stock market, it's a market of stocks. Any company can be out of step with the market, ready to be bought and sold in its own good time.

8

Risk
Management

Men occasionally stumble over the truth, but most of them pick themselves up and hurry off as if nothing happened.

WINSTON CHURCHILL

When an investment opportunity arises, the first question most people ask is, "How much money will I make?" The first question they should ask is, "What is the chance of losing my money—what is the risk involved here?" When there is an acceptable answer to that question, there is an enormously greater chance of reaping—and keeping—a substantial return.

WHY STOCKBROKERS LOVE STATISTICS

You invest $100 in Neon Lights Corp. Within a year the share price doubles, an increase of 100 percent. Suddenly the cost of inert gas goes through the ozone and your stock dives from $200 to $100. Your broker sneers at your complaint. "What are you whining about? You had a 100 percent gain but you had only a 50 percent decline."

"It should be remembered that a decline of 50 percent fully offsets a preceding advance of 100 percent," noted Benjamin Graham.[1]

The notion that risk can be effectively managed has been around for a long time. In fact, in the 1920s Benjamin Graham developed some of the standard hedging techniques that are used today. In recent years, however, risk management has taken on new twists.

THE EFFICIENT MARKET ISN'T

Risk management became a big industry in the past several decades, thanks to the general acceptance of the efficient market hypothesis (EMH). EMH declared that stocks are so efficiently priced by market trading that one investor has very little advantage over another. Creators of the theory maintained that stocks always reflect their future value because investors act quickly on all readily available information. Only investors who are willing to take higher risks can make higher than average returns.

EMH led to an explosion in the futures and options markets, plus the evolution of such fashion plates as portfolio insurance and index arbitrage. These devices seemed necessary for investment managers who attempted to manipulate risk to the very limit to increase a portfolio's return. Paradoxically, it was the linking of portfolio insurance and index arbitrage that accelerated the crash of 1987 and the unlinking of these gimmicks, no doubt, that led to a healthy recovery. Derivatives, another risk management tool, have become infamous for the empires they brought down.

EMH GONE BUT NOT FORGOTTEN

Recent research, plus experiences such as the 1987 crash, has led to the abandonment by most theorists of EMH and its offspring measure of volatility, "beta."

The death of EMH reinforces an old idea. "The moral of all this is simply: There are not rigid mathematical rules that can guarantee success in the stock market. There is only value and the quest for it. That is, an ability to find stocks that are, for one reason or another, cheap in relation to underlying fundamentals and underlying earnings power—and the courage to buy them when you find them," says investment writer David Dreman.[2]

Despite the overwhelming evidence that EMH is invalid, many investment professionals still base their activities on its truth. "Some followers of [EMH] have been willing to get killed in the markets rather than abandon their faith," concludes Dreman.[3]

THE BETA FACTOR

Investment analysts today often measure risk (related to a stock) in terms of volatility, using beta as a measurement. Beta is the covariance of a stock's price movement in relation to the market as a whole. The idea that by understanding and measuring beta an investor could alleviate some investment risk evolved from the efficient market hypothesis. Though much recent research shows that volatility and risk are not related—and even if they were, taking advantage of the knowledge almost always costs more than it saves—many stock rating services still give beta measurements and many investors still desire a low beta. Long before the debunking of beta, value investors were ignoring it as a factor in stock picking.

TURBULENCE DOESN'T MAKE THE FLIGHT DANGEROUS

Beta is irrelevant to a value investor because it is based on short-term stock price movements. The value investor ignores market fluctuations and throws in his lot with intrinsic value. The intrinsic value does not zoom up and down day by day, hour by hour, though price very well may do so. Market activity merely gives the value investor the opportunity to buy or to sell at a chosen price.

Dreman, in a *Forbes* article, explained that he was taking a risky stand when in late 1990 he strongly recommended banks and other financial stocks to the investing public. "These stocks were about as volatile as you can get," Dreman wrote. "Although the stocks had already dropped very sharply, they fell another 10 percent to 15 percent after my recommendations. They then turned around and more than doubled in the next 12 months. Some of the most volatile stocks did far better. PNC and Freddie Mac, for example, were up more than 500 percent in the next few years."

These stocks, Dreman contended, were not excessively risky, despite their volatility. Though the market didn't recognize their value at the time, they were a good buy.

SCREAMINGLY CHEAP STOCKS

"Never mind that the stocks were almost being given away amidst media predictions of impending collapse. The stocks were a steal by any standard but that of [the efficient market hypothesis].... If you buy stocks on your own, forget the widely used risk measurements such as beta. Volatility by itself is no more a gauge of risk in the stock market than it is in making corporate capital spending decisions or the decision of whether to buy or sell a company or business," Dreman said.[4]

Dreman isn't alone in his opinion. "Risk, for value investors, is an adverse change in the intrinsic value of the business," points out Charles Brandes. "The idea then is to keep an eye on the company and not on the stock price."[5]

For a review of the factors that indicate a higher or lower level of risk in a stock, refer to Graham's 10 attributes of an undervalued stock in Chapter 6. Criteria 6 through 10 are indicators of risk.

CONFESSION OF A MONEY MANAGER

Stephen Farley, who runs the Labrador Partners investment fund, in 1995 examined his own portfolio and decided his returns would have been higher had he not engaged in the traditional hedging strategies such as buying "puts" or "calls," depending on whether markets are bearish or bullish.

If he had not hedged, Farley calculated that volatility in his portfolio would have been higher, but so would his average return. His fund reaped a compound average gain of 13.7 percent from 1990 to 1995, versus a gain of 8.7 percent for the Standard & Poor's 500. Without the cost of the puts or calls, he would have had a 16.6 percent return—nearly twice that of the S&P.

Joining the league of other value investors, Farley observed, "Volatility does not equal risk. Had we not hedged, we would have reported more volatile investment results," but better ones.[6] Furthermore, as Peter Lynch points out, hedging can be expensive. "You can waste 5 to 10 percent of your entire investment stake every year to protect yourself from a 5 to 10 percent decline." In most cases, the techniques will cost an individual investor more than they're worth.[7]

Private money managers and individual investors may rethink the practice, and individual investors surely will ignore hedging altogether. For typical investors, it is usually sufficient to simply build in a margin of safety when buying the actual security, and diversifying by filling a portfolio with reasonably priced securities representing many different industries.

However, investment managers with fiduciary responsibility for pension funds and other massive pools of money may very wisely choose to continue to hedge against aberrant market behavior and extreme price declines. Since they may be called upon at any time to return funds to investors, their situation requires a high level of liquidity and extraordinary caution.

For such situations, Graham and Dodd again offer sage advice. Hedging, they say, is an extension of the ordinary concept of investing. It requires knowledge, skill, and discipline.

FUTURES, OPTIONS, AND DERIVATIVES

As mentioned earlier, the lust for higher returns by scientifically managing risk has led to a huge expansion of the futures market. Unusual and arcane derivatives and other stratagems came into use as hedging tools, to the grief of taxpayers in Orange County, California, and others.

In an article written for *Financial Analysts Journal*, Peter L. Bernstein notes, "In a world that is changing faster than any of us can understand, risk seems less amenable to measurement than most investors had come to believe." As a result, he says, some old risk defenses have failed. "An explosive demand for novel forms of containing risk is developing, some of which, I fear, may in the end make markets more risky than less."[8]

A few unusually perceptive investors anticipated problems with derivatives early on. "Warren Buffett thinks that stock futures and options ought to be outlawed, and I agree with him." says Peter Lynch.[9]

Buffett expressed his own point of view: "Derivative transactions are just a little piece of paper between two people that is going to cause one of the two to do something very painful at the end of the period—write a check to the other person. Be sure the person is both willing and able to write the check."[10] Buffett has suggested that the best way to deal with derivatives is to require every chief executive to affirm in his annual report that he understands each derivative contract into which his company has entered.

RISK VERSUS REWARD

Investors are told and told again that when greater risk is involved in an investment, there should be a commensurate possibility of higher reward. There are some cases where the trade-off between risk and reward can be carefully calculated. Venture capitalists, for example, artfully structure their deals to reflect risk.

For the traditional investor, Graham felt that the highest risk came from not having enough time, the right attitude, or the correct information to make investment decisions. Having these elements in place does not eliminate risk, but it does mitigate it:

Investment by nature is not an exact science. The same is true, however, of law and medicine, for here also both individual skill (art) and chance are important factors in determining success or failure. Nevertheless, in these professions analysis is not only useful but indispensable, so that the same should probably be true in the field of investment and possibly in that of speculation."[11]

WHY CASINO OWNERS DON'T DISCUSS STATISTICS

Some cynical individuals, those who may have at one time lost money on their investments, consider investing and gambling to be synonymous. The two are not the same, but the terms *investment*, *speculation*, and *gambling* can be placed on a sliding scale of risk. Investment is at the bottom of the scale, because it allows the greatest degree of knowledge and analysis and the least risk. Speculation comes next on the scale. Though a degree of knowledge and expertise goes into a speculative decision, the speculator realizes that to a great extent, random chance is involved. The speculator recognizes a higher than average possibility of loss. Gambling, on the other hand, is based entirely on random outcomes.

Gamblers play the odds, though unless they own the casino, odds invariably are not in their favor.

Odds are used to determine what advantage favorable chances have over unfavorable chances. These chances can be expressed mathematically. If a penny is tossed in the air, there is equal probability that it will land on heads or tails.

With dice things get more complicated. If you bet that a single die will land on a 6, there is a one-sixth chance that 6 will show its face. There is a five-sixths chance that the die will land on the other five numbers. The odds, then, are 1 in 6 that 6 will appear.

Gamblers sometimes believe the "law of averages" will eventually turn the tide in their favor. Despite its name, the law of averages is not a law. It is what is likely to happen—not what will happen.

Likewise, gamblers are sometimes snared into big losses by the "doctrine of maturity of chances." This is the belief that since an event (the numbers on a bingo card or combination on the roll of dice) have not occurred recently, they are bound to occur soon. What the gambler does not realize is that every chance event is independent of all preceding and following events. The "odds" apply only to that toss of the penny, roll of the dice, or spin of the roulette wheel. They are not cumulative.

The bingo balls don't remember that the B-3 hasn't had a turn recently, nor do the dice remember that the last roll was a 2. This is one characteristic stocks have in common with dice. When warning investors not to get emotionally attached to their stocks, Warren Buffett explains that a stock cannot return your loyalty;

(Don't Discuss Statistics con't) the stock doesn't know you own it.

Yet gamblers who go to Las Vegas and lose shouldn't be too glum. They can think of their losses as a kind of tax that provides cheap buffets, spectacular fantasy hotels, dramatic spewing volcanoes, and glitzy emerald cities for the child within every gambler to enjoy. The gambler's tax also provides employment for many thousands of people and outlandish wealth for several dozen others.

REVISITING SPECULATION

Though virtually every investment carries some level of risk, speculation involves, by definition, a higher level of chance. Various forms of speculation have been presented in this book. Graham's most stringent rule was that any purchase based on anticipated market movements or forecasting or bought with the idea of profiting in a period shorter than the normal business cycle (3 to 5 years) is speculative.

Seth Klarman in his book *Margin of Safety* divides assets and securities into two categories—investments and speculations. While these two categories may appear similar in nature, there is a critical difference: "investments throw off cash for the benefit of the owners; speculations do not."

Klarman's definition eliminates collectibles such as art, furniture, and baseball trading cards as an investment. The only possible return from such acquisitions is a future increase in the price of the object itself. By contrast, a stock's increased price is based on earnings increases. If a stock's price rises on expected earnings increases and those increases don't happen, the higher price is not sustained.[12]

Klarman says that he makes an exception for gold, which is perceived as a storehouse of value. Graham would have categorized gold as a speculation because he argued that gold has lost its effectiveness as a storehouse of value. It is now nothing more than a unique precious metal. Whether investors agree with Klarman or Graham, they are still left with the option of investing in gold-mining shares. Gold mines meet the value investor's criteria because they have the capability of being profitable in and of themselves.

The only problem with value investing in gold-related stocks is that gold has a deeply rooted emotional dimension to it that makes investment objectivity difficult for most people. Gold-related investments are among the most common vehicles of fraud and manipulation around, and have been for hundreds of years.

The value investor's goal is to base investment decisions on fact, not on what is wished for. If risk has a covariable, it is information. The more reliable information an investor has, the less the exposure to risk.

GUESSING VERSUS KNOWING

The value of analysis diminishes as the element of chance increases.[13]

Graham said that there is such a thing as informed speculation. Speculators must consider analysis as an adjunct or an auxiliary rather than as a guide in speculation. It may help increase the chance of winning, but it will not ensure success. Speculators may well have their day, Graham acknowledged, but they also risk taking such a crashing blow that one failure puts them out of business permanently.

"My mentor, Ben Graham, used to say, 'Speculation is neither illegal, immoral, nor fattening (financially)'," Buffett observed.[14]

ALWAYS SOMETHING NEW

One of the things that makes being an investor interesting is that every few years there is a new financial scandal based on speculation and excessive risk taking. The savings and loan fiasco and its link to highly leveraged real estate deals in Texas, California, and other states had a lot in common with the collapse of the fossil fuel industry in Colorado and its connection to highly leveraged commercial real estate deals of a decade earlier. People get excited by the specter of financial gain and join the frenzied crowd. "Like war, speculation is a social activity. It is carried on by groups," observes James Grant.[15]

Sometimes the news stories are nothing more than reruns of old soap operas. Pyramiding, for example, originated with the public utilities and brought down several big companies in the 1920s and 1930s. The

Ponzi took its name from a manipulator nearly 100 years ago, but Ponzi schemes continued to lure investors, Graham and Dodd observed:

> The memory of the financial community is proverbially and distressingly short.[16]

Investors who prefer *not* to be participants in such dramatic stories should protect themselves against risk by:

- Avoiding involvement in products, schemes, or investment vehicles that they do not understand
- Passing up high-risk stocks and bonds
- Avoiding excessive margin

JUNK STOCKS AND BONDS

By paying attention to the balance sheet, income statement, and other quantifiable factors, investors will in almost all cases steer around junk securities of all kinds, no matter how high-yielding they might be. However, Graham taught that if the price is low enough, many otherwise mediocre securities become value buys. It's something like buying a house in a rundown neighborhood. It may not be the ideal purchase, but at a certain price it's still a bargain. It may produce sure rental income, or it may be worth buying simply to fix up and resell at a profit. Deciding if and when a tainted investment has enough potential to take a chance on comes with knowledge and experience. There will be more discussion of this aspect of investing in Chapter 9.

LEVERAGE

When markets are barreling along reaching new highs on a regular basis, it's easy to forget that the racing engine could suddenly die. For those who have overextended their credit, it will be a trying experience. That's exactly how Graham got into trouble in the Crash of 1929.

Months before the crash came, Graham knew that the 1929 market was feverishly overheated, but he believed he'd chosen his stocks wisely. He'd hedged many of his investments. But he also was operating on too much margin, a mistake he dearly paid for and never made again. Graham and his partner, Jerome Newman, worked for 5 years (without compensation) to bring their accounts back to profitable positions. Their clients were thus positioned for the long, steady market climb of the 1930s, 40s, and 50s.

WHEN MARGIN CALLS

Despite the bad experience of the crash, Graham was not dogmatic about leverage. He knew that while there were disadvantages, there also were advantages both for an individual and for a corporation to use credit to finance either portfolio or corporate growth:

> It is clear that leverage is an inherently speculative factor and one that intensifies the possibilities of both gain and loss.[17]

While Graham discouraged small investors from using margin, buying securities on margin does not automatically make an investment unworthy. The investor must be certain that if a margin call comes, it can be met. More importantly, it should be met without jeopardizing the remainder of the portfolio.

Market practices offer some small protection against excessive use of credit purchases. There are strict regulations regarding which securities can be bought on margin and the amount of cash or securities that must be deposited in a margin account. The riskiest of stocks, penny mining stocks, must be bought outright in most cases because nobody can or will lend against them.

BUY A STOCK, AND WATCH THE PRICE FALL

Because a wise investment choice has been made does not mean that the share price of a stock you bought will not temporarily fall below the price at which you purchased it.

What should your reaction as an investor be if a stock declines below your purchase price? Should you have hedged or taken some protective action? Graham says no. A decline in the price of shares does not mean you've actually lost money. If the intrinsic value is there, the price will rise again. If you have confidence in your decision, buy more stock, encourages Charles Brandes.

If an investor believes in dollar cost averaging, to buy when the price has dropped is a true test of that belief. It's easy to keep buying while the share price is rising; it takes fortitude to do so when the price is declining.

CONCLUSION

Value investors may decide to enter a speculative investment venture, but not without full knowledge of the risk that is taken. There is such a thing as intelligent speculation.

Risk management is built into the concepts of value investing. The three legs on which the concept is built—avoidance of speculation, margin of safety, and diversification—provide inexpensive and easy-to-use tools for risk management. The investor who understands these concepts will sleep well at night, even when Mr. Market is in one of his most agitated moods.

IN THE MEANTIME, REMEMBER

- "Beware lest you lose the substance by grasping at the shadow." Aesop's Fables. Investor's corollary: "Hold on to the substance (investment principle) and the shadow (investment return) will follow."

- The measurement of risk in terms of market volatility (beta) is of no importance to the value investor. A high-beta stock is no riskier than a low-beta stock.

- An investment throws off cash for the benefit of the investor. A speculation does not.

- The best hedge for individual investors is informed decisions, margin of safety, and diversification.

- The best way to improve your luck is to stop gambling. Start investing instead.

9

Special Circumstances

Innovation is the life force of the financial markets, and ortho-doxy for its own sake avails nothing except nostalgia.[1]

JAMES GRANT

Value investing is nothing if it's not vigilant. Both *Security Analysis and The Intelligent Investor* contain admonitions of watchfulness and abundant "thou shalt nots." But Graham taught that with information, practice, and experience, vigilance serves more than to keep investors out of hot water. It alerts them to "special circumstances." It allows value investors to achieve exceptional yields without adding undue or unnecessary risk.

Special circumstances, or the nontraditional opportunities to reap an unusually high investment return, are difficult to describe, since by definition they are rare, offbeat, and inventive and in many cases their occurrence cannot be anticipated.

Special circumstances can come about in many ways. Often they are a unique and surprising path by which a security works its way to intrinsic value. Sometimes they are the "exception" that every rule is supposed to have. When an investor finds a special circumstance, the "thou shalts" overthrow the "thou shalt nots."

AMENDING THE RULES

Graham short-circuited two of his own rules when in 1948 he bought controlling interest in the Government Employees Insurance Co. (Geico).

In a postscript to the fourth revision of *The Intelligent Investor*, Graham told the story of two partners "whom we know very well" who violated their own portfolio guidelines by putting a larger percentage of their total investment pool into a single company (one-fifth of the Graham Newman Fund) and by settling for fewer tangible assets than they ordinarily would have, because in every other way the company looked like a winner. And Geico was:

> Ironically enough, the aggregate of profits accruing from this single investment decision far exceeded the sum of all the others realized through 20 years of wide-ranging operation in the partners' specialized fields, involving much investigation, endless pondering, and countless individual decisions.[2]

Which only goes to show, said Graham, "that there are several different ways to make and keep money in Wall Street."[3]

WHEN OPPORTUNITY KNOCKS, CHECK ITS ID

A special circumstance, in Graham parlance, is a situation that may appear unusual, unorthodox, or even overvalued, but upon steely-eyed evaluation, contains abundant intrinsic value. It is just too good to pass up. As Graham often repeated, even an ordinary investment can have great value at the right price.

Geico qualified as a special circumstance, though one that the ordinary investor may never encounter. At the time the Graham Newman Fund bought a controlling interest, Geico was a privately owned company. (The full Geico story is recounted in the Appendix.)

Geico again surfaced as a quasi-special circumstance in 1995. At that time Berkshire Hathaway made a $2.3 billion offer to purchase the 48 percent of the company it did not already own. It was presumed Warren Buffett was utilizing some of the cash his company received from the sale of Cap Cities/ABC to Walt Disney. Buffett actually accepted Disney stock as payment. He used cash generated from his own business to acquire this bargain from his own backyard.

The field of special circumstances can involve highly undervalued common shares, convertible securities, preferred stocks, and warrants; various arbitrage scenarios; bankruptcies; junk bonds, initial public offerings, spinoffs, private deals, and both arcane and complex legal situations. Quite often, by contemplating all aspects of an unusual business development, the lucrative upside jumps right off the page, it is so obvious.

ULTRA-UNDERVALUED STOCKS

This class of securities has been discussed in previous chapters. Undervalued companies become "special circumstance" stocks when they are selling at such a low price as to be exceptionally attractive, and seemingly involve an extra level of risk. Often the company's shares are low priced because it is in serious trouble.

In the 1940 edition of *Security Analysis* Graham published two lists of exceptionally low-priced special investment situations. In the 8 years following the publication of that edition, the stocks on the two lists advanced an average of 252 percent, compared with a 33 percent rise in the Standard & Poor's industrials.

Many of these companies were suffering from the Great Depression and a world war that already had ignited in Europe. Though the companies survived those episodes of history, it is interesting to note how many of the companies are now extinct. On the list were Reo, Hudson, Hupp, and Nash Motors, all automobile manufacturers. The list also included brand names that have survived and are prospering today such as Mack Truck, Diamond Match, Montgomery Ward, and Wesson Oil.

In Chapter 5, we looked at Oak Industries, which at one time in the late 1980s was selling below $1 per share and was so far below its asset value that it became a compelling purchase, despite the company's blundering ways.

WORKOUTS

One of Warren Buffett's favorite special circumstances is what he calls "workouts." "These are securities whose financial results depend on corporate action, rather than on supply and demand factors created by buyers and sellers of securities. In other words, they are securities with a timetable where we can predict, with reasonable error limits, when we will get and how much and what might upset the apple cart," Buffett explained.[4]

Takeover arbitrage, bankruptcy arbitrage, the spinoff of a company into an independent corporation, or even taking a public company private can present a workout investment.

CONVERTIBLES WITH THE TOP DOWN

Convertible securities most often are bonds, but they also can be preferred stocks. They are truly convertible because at some point in their life, they can be exchanged for a set number of common shares. The price of the convertible tends to track the company's common stock price as the market rises. But because the bond or preferred pays a coupon rate higher than the common stock dividend, convertibles don't decline as much in a down market.

For this reason, professional investors prefer convertibles over common stock in a high-risk atmosphere. When stocks are trading at historically high price levels, convertibles allow the investor to capture much of the upward momentum of the common stock, and to lose less of it if the market reverses. As a result, an investor can get close to the same total return as she would get on the company's common stock, but at lower risk.

Because of the way these securities are structured and because there is a "convertible premium" based on the higher yield, it rarely pays to convert a bond to the stock.

AMERICAN AIRLINES CONVERTIBLE BONDS

	Current	Price	Scenario 1*	Scenario 2*
	Yield	4/27/95	Stock -28% in 1 year	Stock +39% in 1 year
Common Stock	0%	$68	$49 (-28%)	$95 (+39%)
Convertible Bond	6.26%	$98	$85 (-6.5%)	$121 (+30%)

*Stock's potential movement based on its historical volatility.

Source: *Business Week*, May 15, 1995, p. 148.

PREFERRED STOCKS

Preferred stocks are a hybrid security. Like common stocks, they represent ownership in the company, but they carry a set rate of return that must be paid ahead of the common stock dividend. Even if the preferred dividend is suspended, it accumulates and takes precedence over future common stock dividends. For this reason preferred shares should be seen as similar to and evaluated like a corporate bond.

Because investors buy preferred stock for the yield, it is paramount that the company have the wherewithal to pay the promised dividend. The company's debt should be within manageable bounds and its earnings should be sufficient to cover both its bond and its preferred obligations. (For the appropriate level of earnings coverage for bonds, refer to the section in this chapter on junk bonds.)

When preferred stocks are convertible or have warrants attached, the investor must also think about the intrinsic value of the common shares. Because convertibles are good only if the share price increases, a value investor must consider earnings when evaluating them. As a general rule, investors do not intend to convert, but when the market takes unusual turns, it can become the right thing to do. There will be more discussion on warrants in the next section.

Buffett invested in both Salomon Inc. and U.S. Air by purchasing preferred stock. The purpose of the investment was to reap the dividends. U.S. Air paid a substantial part of its preferred dividend, but in the first quarter of 1995 Berkshire finally wrote down $268.5 million, or 75 percent of its investment. Buffett explained that the write-down was taken to recognize that the decline in the value of the U.S. Air investment was "other than temporary."

Though Salomon met its dividend obligation, the investment bank caused Buffett more work and worry than he may have chosen. (He was compelled to fly in from Omaha to run the New York investment banking house as it worked its way out of trouble with the SEC for a little catalog of misdeeds.) Still, there were benefits. Buffett acquired $700 million in Salomon preferreds in 1987. The shares paid a 9 percent dividend, which dumped $63 million a year into Berkshire Hathaway's bank account. The income also had a tremendous tax advantage, since corporations don't pay taxes on 70 percent of dividend income earned from preferred stocks.

Berkshire could convert the first of five lots of the Salomon convertible preferreds into common stock at $38 per share at any time before October 31, 1995, or redeem the shares for cash. Buffett converted the shares to cash, signaling to the investment world that either he had little confidence in Salomon's long-term success or that he thought the shares were overvalued at $38.

WARRANTS

Warrants are securities that usually are issued together with a bond or preferred stock. The warrant entitles the investor to buy a proportionate amount of common stock at a specified price, most likely higher than the market price at the time of issuance. The investor thus is able to keep the fixed-income investment but also has the opportunity to benefit from stock price appreciation.

Warrants often are used as a sweetener in special financing situations, such as to augment the appeal of a fixed-income security. They are especially popular in restructuring a troubled company or issuing new shares for a weak one. They seem to many investors like something a little extra.

Warrants are in name and in form, as low-priced stocks frequently are in essence, a long-term call upon the future of a business. In other words, warrants dilute the value of all the common stock. An investor must assume warrants will be exercised whenever figuring the number of shares outstanding for a company, but not count them as worth much when considering the value of the sponsoring bond or preferred. View a warrant something like a speculative senior security, says *Security Analysis*.[5]

Warrants, Graham and Dodd note, are dangerously usable in a manipulative way. When evaluating warrants, the desirable factors are:

• A low price
• A long duration
• An option or purchase price close to the market price

As a conservative rule of thumb, the investor should pay nothing extra for warrants, and if they turn out to be of value, then the pot indeed has been sweetened.

ARBITRAGE AU NATURAL

In the early 1990s as Russia was just yanking off the hood of communism, a retired hairdresser noted that clothes cost more at a street market near her own home than they did at the market across Moscow, near her daughter's house. She withdrew 2000 rubles from her savings, bought a pile of clothes at the cheap market, and resold them for 3000 rubles at the market near her home. With no outside lessons in capitalism, she discovered arbitrage.[6]

Arbitrage—the buying of a security at one price with the intention of reselling it quickly at a higher price—is a way for professional investors to make money fast. Arbitrage can involve a merger, a takeover, or in extreme circumstances, the purchase of a company and liquidation of its assets.

Arbitrage is "simple in both conception and execution, but opportunities are few," explained the British magazine *The Economist.*[7]

LIQUIDATION ARBITRAGE

Graham first made a name for himself on Wall Street in 1915 (he was just 21 years old) when he studied a plan for the dissolution of the Guggenheim Exploration Company. He spotted a classic setup for liquidation arbitrage. Guggenheim was a holding company with large interests in several copper-mining companies that were trading on the New York Stock Exchange. Graham figured the company's assets this way:

		Market Value Sept. 1, 1915
One share of Guggenheim Exploration		$68.88
Securities Owned by Guggenheim		
.7277 share, Kennecott Copper @ 52.50	=	38.20
.1172 share Chino Copper @ 46.00	=	5.39
.0833 share American Smelting @ 81.75	=	6.81
.185 share Ray Consolidated Copper @ 22.88	=	4.23
Other assets	=	21.60
Total	=	$76.23

This simple math showed that buying Guggenheim at $68.88 and collecting the proceeds from the liquidation (at $76.23 per share) would yield an arbitrage profit of $7.35 per share. A profit of 10.7 percent in a matter of months was a splendid prospect.

There was risk, of course—the risk that shareholders might disapprove the dissolution; that the price of the underlying shares would decline before the dissolution was complete; or that litigation might intervene. Even so, Graham's company agreed to take an arbitrage position in Guggenheim, and the dissolution went through very much as young Graham expected it would.[8]

TAKEOVER OR MERGER ARBITRAGE

Value investors often are confronted with the possibility of participating in merger, acquisition, or takeover activity, by virtue of the very fact that they've bought undervalued stocks. The aggressor company saw the same undervaluation of assets that the investor did. Acquiring an undervalued company is an easy way to grow assets, sales, or market share at a relatively low price.

When merger mania hits Wall Street, as it did in the summer of 1995, there are winners and losers, and winners who feel like losers because their take wasn't as much as they had hoped for. The chance of disappointment is especially high for arbitrageurs who buy shares solely to benefit if a rumored takeover offer comes about.

Those investors who placed advance bets that Upjohn, a small and undervalued U.S. pharmaceuticals company, would be snapped up at a lofty price were among the disappointed. Upjohn instead arranged a cooperative merger with Pharmacia, a European medicines manufacturer. The deal gave the companies a possible $500 million annually in cost savings and was expected to add 65 cents per share to annual earnings of the combined companies.

Even though the merger would make both companies stronger and more competitive in the marketplace, Wall Streeters began referring to the company as "Downjohn" and the deal as a "takeunder." The merger arbitrageurs hoped for hot competitive bidding that would drive the share price much higher. They were not satisfied with holding the shares of a company with greatly improved earnings prospects. Arbitrageurs like to make money faster than the normal earnings progression provides.

SURPRISE PACKAGES

The best special-circumstance deals often are those that arrive unexpectedly. With a sharp eye for undervalue, an investor can be at the scene ahead of the arbitrageur. Anyone who owned software developer Lotus before International Business Machines announced a blowout bid fared handsomely. The offering price was nearly double the share price at which Lotus had been trading. IBM initially offered $60 per share but went to $64 before the acquisition was consummated. The Lotus offer was made just as IBM was emerging from a decade-long restructuring that sunk IBM's own share price to record low levels.

Lotus displayed many of the symptoms of a temporarily troubled company that might make a good long-term value buy. In 1994 Lotus was regrouping after reporting its first loss (following a $68 million charge related to acquisitions). Its revenues were off after a mistaken judgment by management on the success of Windows, software to which Lotus products should have been keyed early on. Additionally, some of Lotus's own new software got off to a slow start and sales suffered that year. Lotus's share price dove from a high of 86.5 in 1994 to a low of 25 in 1995.

Yet viewed over the past 10 years, Lotus's sales had grown at 30.5 percent per year and its earnings at 15 percent. Despite gloomy company news, working capital was still strong and its current ratio was still a healthy 2.5. As for qualitative factors, Lotus's management had provided strong leadership and steady growth over a long period of time—an especially long time, considering the speed of developments in the computer software universe.

Lotus qualified for purchase using the intrinsic value formula, even without allowances for its growth stock status. With 1994 earnings of $1.08, an expected growth rate of 16 percent, and an average bond yield of 7.37 percent, the formula works out this way:

$$E(2R + 8.5) \times 4.4 / Y$$
Or
$$\$1.08 \ (2 \times 16\% + 8.5) \times 4.4 / 7.37 = \$26.11$$

In other words the shares were trading near their quantitative intrinsic value when IBM made its offer of more than double that amount. Obviously IBM took qualitative factors into consideration as well when it made its calculations.

The dynamics of IBM/Lotus are complicated, but the principle is simple. If an investor had identified Lotus as a value investment, bought the shares, then waited for the story to play out . . . you get the picture. That's why patient value investors enjoy exceptional long-term profits.

MERGERS OF EQUALS

Arbitrage profits are easiest to evaluate and often the most enriching for the value investor when there is a cash offer for the shares of the target company. When the deal is a stock swap or a "merger of equals," it is then necessary to evaluate the new or postmerger company. If the newly formed company still qualifies as a good value, keep it. If not—if, for example, the deal is overburdened with debt or offers no economies of scale or cost-cutting by streamlining overlapping areas of interest—collect profits and step briskly along to the next value investment.

Selling is always safer than staying. If the investors sells, it may be possible to capture profits and to do so quickly. If the investor stays in, benefits may take time to evolve, assuming they ever evolve.

THE LAWS OF ARBITRAGE

Arbitrage issues usually sell at 1 to 5 percent below the proposed takeover price, reflecting uncertainties over whether the deal will go through or it will be stalled for so long that either the fundamentals change or the chance for a quick profit is lost. Arbitrageurs hope to make 5 percent on capital within a few months.

In arbitrage look for:

- Large discounts from takeover price
- Friendly offers
- Easy financing
- Reasonable takeover price compared with the value of the company
- Expected annualized rate of return, minimum of 25 to 30 percent

Less well-known companies are better candidates for takeover arbitrage because competition is lighter. During his time as an investment manager, Graham made large amounts of money in arbitrage. Today, with so many arbitrage players crowding the field, the share price moves more quickly and closer to the offering price, thus closing down the time frame in which an arbitrage position can be established.

BANKRUPTCIES

When bad things happen to good companies, many dash for the protection of the bankruptcy court to reorganize. Two things occur when any public company enters Chapter 11 (reorganization) bankruptcy.

- The company is protected from creditors until it works out its difficulties, if that is possible.
- The share price takes a nose dive and often, bond prices fall below face value.

If a company cannot haul itself out of Chapter 11 bankruptcy, it proceeds to dissolution. The assets are sold. Creditors, including bondholders even if the bonds are in default, are paid off. Any remaining money is returned to shareholders. Even if the bond eventually goes into default, if there are enough assets to cover debt, the bondholder eventually should be paid.

For this reason, successful bankruptcy arbitrage requires attention to the company's tangible assets. Two conditions must exist for a bankrupt company to qualify as a special-circumstance investment:

- A large margin of safety, as measured by assets
- A strong likelihood that the company will emerge from bankruptcy

When asset value is high enough and stock or bond price is low enough, investors have a margin of safety whether or not the company survives. Values that extreme are unusual even in bankruptcy, however, and it is always preferable if a company can rebound. For one thing, dissolution, when it occurs, seems to take forever to reach completion. If and when the company emerges from bankruptcy, its debt obligation will have been satisfied in some way, and the share price is primed for a dramatic recovery.

JUNK BONDS

Junk bonds often are just like the stuff that you might find at a garage sale—tired goods of questionable value. Yet as any streetwise shopper knows, treasures can rest among the discards. This author met a man who in 1995 found a first edition of *Security Analysis* at a garage sale. He bought it for $1. A first edition that is in good condition, when it can be found, sells for more than $1000. To the seller and to most unaware shoppers, however, the book was old junk.

What is junk in financial terms? Junk bonds are debt securities of less than investment grade. These bonds carry a rating of BB or lower by a rating agency. By accepted standards of safety, industrial companies should have earnings, before taxes, of 5 times interest expense. Junk bond issues usually have coverage of pretax earnings of only 1.3 times interest expense, and often less than that.

While junk bonds gained fame as a gimmick to make Michael Milken rich from fees he charged investors, other canny investors also have made money in this field.

EXCUSE ME?

The investment world was shaken in 1983 when Washington Public Power Service defaulted on $2.2 billion worth of bonds that had been floated to finance its nuclear power plant Projects 4 and 5. The company earned the nickname "Whoops." The shock spread from the Northwest to the Midwest when in Berkshire Hathaway's 1985 annual report Buffett revealed that he had purchased $139 million worth of bonds in WPPS Projects 1, 2, and 3.

The bonds' special appeal? Because of the company's default stigma, Buffett could buy the bonds at a steep discount. Nevertheless, the bonds were supported by underlying assets. Berkshire earned a fixed 16.3 percent tax-free current yield from the securities—a $22.7 million annual return on the investment.

Though Buffett does not care for bonds, he has a history of buying them when they offer exceptional advantage. In the 1970s he bought shaky Chrysler bonds and Penn Central for 50 cents on the dollar. In 1989 and 1990, he bought the junk bonds of R. J. R. Nabisco.[9]

When considering the purchase of a low-rated bond because its price is astoundingly cheap, look to the survivability of the issuer. A bond cannot be of better quality than the assets and earnings of the company that issues it. Yet the fact that bond holders get in line ahead of shareholders in the case of liquidation can be taken as a plus.

INITIAL PUBLIC OFFERINGS

While institutions and professional money managers can sometimes make outstanding profits on initial public offerings, it is difficult for an individual to buy stock at its offering price. Institutions can place orders for blocks of shares in advance, whereas individuals, except in special cases, cannot. When a stock comes on the market with enormous fanfare, a relatively small number of shares are allocated to individuals, known as retail investors. Once the offering starts, share price usually rises very quickly, and individuals are left to buy in the rising market. Once IPO fever has burned off, the price invariably declines.

Some IPO investors hope to buy shares early at a low price and then sell them quickly for a profit while enthusiasm for the new stocks is high. Brokers call this "flipping," and are likely to balk at clients who try it. The brokers often are charged commission penalties for clients who try to take quick profits from IPO trading patterns.

IPOs have a tainted reputation as an investment, and not without cause. Research shows that ordinarily if you buy an IPO and hold it for 5 years, your average annual return would be a skimpy 5 percent per year. Most of the IPO profits come within the first 90 days the shares are traded. Obviously despite the reluctance of brokers, some clients manage to get in and out with lucky timing.[10]

On the other hand, some young public companies have been phenomenal long-term investments. For example, in the decade after it went public, Home Depot's annual return was 32,143 percent. In its first 8 years, Blockbuster Video appreciated 9375 percent. In 11 years Liz Claiborne rose 5722 percent. These companies started with track records, strong fundamentals, and good growth prospects.[11]

Despite the near certainty of high volatility in the first year, value investors should be on the alert for initial public offerings of solid, promising companies. Evaluation of the company is much the same as it is for any stock. In addition to looking for an acceptable price-to-earnings ratio, debt-to-equity ratio, and other numbers, an IPO investor should:

- Examine the fees charged by underwriters for the offering. Those fees have to be paid first before future earnings go back into the company or to shareholders. It is sometimes the case that fees are so high the new shareholder has little chance of profit for many years to come.

- Ask how the company will use the capital it raises. If the money is used to reduce debt or expand the business, for example, investors are likely to benefit.

- Check to see how much of the offering will be used to buy out the existing owners. If the offering is just an opportunity for founders to cash out, the new investor should ask why the founders want out of this company if its prospects are so hot.

If an investor finds an IPO with solid credentials, and by luck can get in at the offering price, so much the better. Underwriters who take companies public traditionally price the shares a little below their intrinsic value. They want the company to raise as much money in the offering as possible, but investors would feel cheated if the stock sold at a low price but never rose at all.

One reason IPOs are difficult investments is that companies go public when markets are high, if they can, in an attempt to raise the largest pool of capital possible. The bull market presents these high prices, called a "window of opportunity." When the market chills down, the share prices of recent public offerings frequently contract.

PENNY STOCKS

New investors too often confuse special circumstances with penny stock deals. These very low-priced (usually under $5) stocks are typically sold from over-the-counter pink sheets, from the Vancouver (Canada) Stock Exchange, or from some obscure foreign exchange. Often the tip-off is that the company is peddling a promising, socially redeeming technology, or a rare or high-priced commodity.

Gold, silver, and precious gem-mining and oil-drilling ventures can be notoriously overinflated. The objective of operators on the Vancouver Stock Exchange—where such issues are rampant—is to get in early with the promoters and get out while the price is artificially high, playing in the game of the promoters themselves. This is gambling in its crudest form. Graham and Dodd warned:

The public would do well to remember that whenever it becomes easy to raise capital for a particular industry, both the chances of unfair deals are magnified and the danger of overdevelopment of the industry itself becomes very real.[12]

CONCLUSION

When evaluating investments that qualify as "special," investors need to do extra homework and engage in a severely critical evaluation process. When a deal sounds too good to be true, it usually is. Fortunately, however, special circumstances do occur, and when they crop up, a seasoned, level-headed investor will celebrate the best of them. Stock markets are made fascinating by the amazing things that occur there.

"To suppose that the value of a common stock is determined purely by a corporation's earnings discounted by the relevant interest rates and adjusted for the marginal tax rate is to forget that people have burned witches, gone to war on a whim, risen to the defense of Joseph Stalin, and believed Orson Welles when he told them over the radio that the Martians had landed," said James Grant.[13]

IN THE MEANTIME, REMEMBER

- Investment rules are written to be studied, then tailored to the circumstances. "Most men would rather die than change. Many have," wrote Bertrand Russell. Value investors *can* change when necessary.
- Watch for banner headlines for special-circumstance opportunities. Bankruptcies, defaults, and corporate catastrophes make big news, and they set the stage for bargains. When a company's reputation or credit has been damaged, it must pay a premium for new money.

- The value of warrants, like that of options, is derived at the expense of the common stock.

- Special-circumstance investments must have intrinsic value and the value should be fairly visible. "We never sat down and wrote down the formula. We do it in our heads. We like the decision to be obvious enough that we don't have to run numbers," said Warren Buffett.[14]

The Truth Shall Make You Wealthy

Value Investing is just standard economics. Think logically about what you're doing. Think about it without emotion. And think about what makes sense.[1]

ANDREW WEISS

A n investor who is famous for ragging on his broker whenever the market turns against him told a friend that value investing, to him, was like watching the grass grow. "Perhaps," replied the friend, "but the value investors I know watch the grass grow at the best country clubs in the world."

If someone comes into the market looking for entertainment, there is plenty of action to be found. If an investor hopes to accumulate wealth with limited risk, that also is possible. There is no need to demand volumes of academic studies, page after page of charts, or the clamoring crowd of investment advisers who want a percentage of your money, whether it has earned an acceptable return or not. An individual can successfully manage his or her own money using value investing principles. It is even possible to structure a high-return, virtually permanent portfolio.

Many investors who discover value investing are like the man who studied for years for the priesthood, to discover that all he needed to know was the Ten Commandments, claims Warren Buffett.

FOLLOW THOSE WHO DO BEST

The most convincing proof that value investing works is the number of high-performing investment managers and financial analysts who have followed the course. "I would figure that anyone starting out would look at what's been successful over time and try to duplicate it. It amazes us that so few people actually do this," said Buffett.[2]

VALUE INVESTING CONDENSED

Nevertheless, there is a congregation of faithful disciples who believe that all an investor has to do is identify undervalued stocks, buy them and hold them until they have appreciated to overvalue, then sell for a profit. If the stock continues to demonstrate the promise of accruing value in the future, it can be held indefinitely within a portfolio. Unlike speculators, value investors buy stocks as if they were buying the whole business, advised Graham:

> True investors can exploit the recurrent excessive optimism and excessive apprehension of the speculative public.[3]

True value investors are rare, but there are some in each generation who see the light. "I will admit to being a convert to this approach and, as with many converts, I am deeply committed to it," explains money manager Charles Brandes. "I have seen the results; I know it works; and I know it will build wealth for those who apply its principles."[4]

THE SIMPLER THE BETTER

While Graham's investing methods made money for him and most of his students, he experimented throughout his life trying to improve upon his techniques and refine his knowledge. When he was 82 years old, he summed up a lifetime of research:

> I think we can (invest) successfully with a few techniques and simple principles. The main point is to have the right general principles and the character to stick to them.[5]

BEYOND BEN GRAHAM

Computers: It seems perfectly logical that the principles of Graham and Dodd should easily lend themselves to the computerized selections of stocks. So far, however, no investment gurus have successfully adapted their teachings to the electronic medium.

Benjamin Graham had no use for computers, and though Warren Buffett uses one to play bridge with friends in far-off places, he does not rely on a computer to invest. The careers of both these men began (and Graham's finished) during times when computers were fairly rough instruments.

Though it is clear that a computer cannot replace human judgment, if Graham had been born in a different era, he may very well have been attracted to computers. Many professional and individual investors are using them extensively as a tool.

Graham may have found them useful in four ways:

- Gathering information on companies

- Record keeping—storing specific stock and portfolio information

- Tracking portfolio performance

- Crunching numbers—but this is the siren's song

Somehow it's easy to believe that if you just put in enough numbers, a software program can make better decisions than you can. The computer can't make final decisions. It has no way of dealing with qualitative factors. The computer, however, is an excellent manipulator, storehouse, and presenter of data. Professional investors will find a wealth of computer databases, screening programs, and other investment products that are or can be tailored specifically to his or her goals. They are costly, but for those managing millions of dollars, such sophisticated programs often prove useful.

Both professional and dedicated individual investors will find useful information and time-saving features in over-the-counter purchased software, on-line brokerages, general on-line services such as Prodigy, CompuServe, Genie, and America OnLine, and finally the Internet.

There is an advantage to purchasing investment software and storing it in your computer's memory. When you have the software you need, you don't have to go on-line, or connect via a modem, telephone, and fee-based service of some kind to do your work. Assuming you already have a computer, the cost is simply the price of the software itself.

(Beyond Ben Graham con't)

However, if you want to check current stock prices, do trading via computer, or have the computer continually track portfolio changes, you will need to go on-line by connecting your computer to some outside source using your telephone and a modem. You may also find on-line stock research services to be valuable.

Programs that can help you set up your portfolio, track changes, buy and sell stocks, and so forth are available through a wide range of both well-known and obscure sources. Charles Schwab, Fidelity Investments, Quick & Reilly, and other discount brokers have captured the lead in this field, but competitors join their ranks daily.

One of the less complicated ways to access large amounts of investment information is to subscribe to an on-line service. Most on-line companies offer similar services, though they may be presented in different ways, using different colors and graphics and sporting different catchy names. For example, America OnLine's (AOL) offerings are far-reaching, and most but not all of the information is useful to dedicated investors. It depends on your temperament and your investment goals.

AOL and most of its competitors have both news and feature article services from leading newspapers and magazines. News is updated on an hourly basis. There are offerings of economic and market predictions of every sort. Mutual fund investors will find many different sources of information, some provided by mutual fund companies themselves. However, MorningStar and other independent information services are on-line. There are numerous "chat rooms" in the financial area, in which members are invited to ask questions and discuss issues. Quite often the questions and answers are trivial, mundane, or way off base for a value investor. When asking a question, participants have no idea who will answer and what credentials that person has. Investors claim, however, that they often get good information, sometimes from employees of the company under discussion, from the chat rooms.

The best way to measure a service's usefulness is to enroll for a month (most give free extra hours in the first month) and hack around. Explore and try things out.

Here is how I use AOL. I've set up an AOL portfolio listing my stocks. It was easy to log into the Quotes and Portfolio area and follow the on-screen instructions. Now, any time of the day or night I want to check price changes for a specific holding or the value of individual stocks or the total portfolio, all I do is log on and pull up my portfolio file. The portfolio's

(Beyond Ben Graham con't)
total value, with prices as current as 15 minutes ago, pops onto the screen. The appreciation of each stock since purchase is listed. I can quickly download the full portfolio onto my own computer so that I can look at it when I'm not logged on to AOL.

When I'm considering buying or selling a stock, I look it up in Hoover Company Profiles. Hoover provides a corporate history, description of the business, list of officers, income statements and balance sheets, and the stock's trading history. PC Financial provides an annual report service.

Occasionally the information I find is too stale or too limited to be useful. In that case, I use AOL to access the Internet, where I find the Securities and Exchange Commission's Edgar information service. Edgar allows free access to SEC corporate reports that in the past were available only by expensive or time-consuming methods. Unfortunately, only reports of those corporations that file electronically are available. As of mid-1995 only about 8500 of the nearly 15,000 publicly traded companies were filing electronically and therefore available on Edgar. However, the number of companies filing reports electronically is increasing quickly. The largest, most prominent, and most actively traded companies were first to

go on-line, so the likelihood of finding a 10-K, proxy, or other document for the most interesting companies is good.

When I've done my company research (and downloaded into my own computer the reports I want to keep), I can then check the price through the Quotes and Portfolio service. Again, there is a 15-minute delay from the actual market price, but that's close enough for anyone other than a day trader.

Several brokerages offer on-line trading accounts, as do some computer-only trading firms. PC Financial Network is one of the largest services. CompuServe advertises E*Trade, which specializes in over-the-counter and NASDAQ trades. Though my discount broker, Quick & Reilly, allows on-line trading through AOL and CompuServe, I don't use it. The company offers a deeper discount for trading by touchtone telephone. (A value investor trims costs wherever possible.)

AOL and its competitors offer another service that many investors will like—a review of investment software and the opportunity to download it for a nominal fee. The variety of software is dazzling. There are charting programs for figuring mortgage payments and amortization; for fundamental portfolio management; Buffett Stock Evaluation Models; growth stock

(Beyond Ben Graham con't)
spreadsheets; and programs for technical analysis. As is so often the case with so-called shareware, the user may find it isn't compatible with his or her own software, but when it is, this can be a convenient way to acquire programs.

Information services such as AOL and CompuServe are considered less than cool by those who are tuned into that vast worldwide jumble of information, the Internet. The Internet is interesting, but not as wonderful for investors as it sounds. Many "home pages" are self-serving, put there by government agencies, companies, or brokerage houses to tout themselves. Megabytes of sales hype, "flame jobs," and general trash are loaded on the Internet daily. For example, when searching for information on Coca Cola, I found a large file under that title, and enthusiastically downloaded it, thinking it must be important stuff. Instead it was a vague but vitriolic, anti-Coca Cola graphic. It's frustrating to waste 10 minutes on a meaningless exercise when you're paying by the minute to be logged on.

In addition, the Internet has increasingly become an underworld for stock hustlers, promoters and manipulators. Wheeler-dealers who once worked from telephone boiler rooms are catching many pigeons on the Internet.

High-tech and software stocks especially appeal to the computer-oriented people who regularly surf the Net. They've heard many tales of instant 16-year-old software millionaires, and this sets them up for easy scamming. The dangers aren't severe enough to keep investors off the net, however.

The following Internet (or the segment referred to as the World Wide Web, WWW) addresses will help investors find trustworthy information:

- Corporate and mutual fund SEC filings—
  http://town.hall.org/edgar/edgar.html

- Stock quotes on a 15-minute delay—
  http://www.secapl.com/cgi-bin/qs

- List of WWW "home pages" maintained by public companies—
  http://networth.galt.com/www/home/insider/public-co.html

At this time, the best thing about Internet is the SEC's Edgar, which is described above. However, the Internet changes constantly. All an investor can do is "surf the net" from time to time so as not to be left out.

But beware. Investing via computer can become an obsession, an end unto itself. Much time can be spent browsing and download-

(Beyond Ben Graham con't) ing information you don't want or need. Much money can be spent on hardware, software, and endless computer gadgets. Day-by-day, minute-by-minute tracking of performance is fascinating, but it can be anxiety-making and lead to overactive trading.

There is so much to see and do on-line that an investor can lose sight of the objective—to make money in the investment markets.

THREE PILLARS

Graham preached easy commandments that any investor can use as stars when navigating the expansive seas of the investment world. An individual investor, who isn't under pressure to shoot comets across the heavens but would like to earn healthy and sustainable returns, especially can benefit from Graham's guidance. Value investing is more of a philosophy than a technique. It cannot be represented by a single formula or checklist. It is based on the idea that an investor is searching for bargain stocks, and there are several ways of recognizing them. Graham's philosophy is built on three pillars:

• *Investment approach.* Have the attitude of an investor, not a speculator:

Let us define the speculator as one who seeks to profit from market movements, without primary regard to intrinsic values. The prudent stock investor is one who (a) buys only at prices amply supported by underlying value, and (b) determinedly reduces his stock holdings when the market enters the speculative phase of a sustained advance.[6]

Educated speculation, Graham insisted, has a place in the securities markets, but a speculator must do deeper research, track investments, and be prepared for losses when they come:

If a man wants to make lots of money speculating, he must have a pretty good reason to believe he's smarter than the next guy. Lucky he is if he actually turns out to be.[7]

- *Margin of safety.* This is an evasive but important concept. "There is simply no precision to the process—and if you think so, you are kidding yourself," advises Warren Buffett. "There should be such a margin of safety that you don't need to carry it out to three decimal places."[8]

- *Intrinsic value.* "Intrinsic value is importantly influenced by what you do with capital over time. Intrinsic value is more than simply adding up the pieces at the time," Buffett adds.[9]

CHECKPOINTS

In greatly simplified terms, here are additional points Graham emphasized in his writing and speaking. Some of the counsel is technical, but much of it simply encourages the right attitude.

- *Know the asking price.* Multiply the company's share price by the number of total shares (undiluted) outstanding. Ask yourself, "If I bought the whole company would it be worth this much money?" Compare the asking price with that of other companies whose stock seem suitable for purchase.

- *Continually search for bargains.* Graham is best known for using his net current asset value (NCAV) rule to decide if a company is worth its market price. By purchasing stocks below NCAV, the investor buys a bargain, because nothing is paid for fixed assets. Research shows that buying stocks immediately after their price drops below NCAV per share, and selling the shares within 2 years, provides an average excess return of over 24 percent.

Yet even Graham recognized that NCAV stocks are increasingly difficult to find, and when such a stock is located, this measure is only a starting point:

If the investor has occasion to be fearful of the future of such a company, it is perfectly logical for him to obey his fears and pass on from that enterprise to some other security about which he is not so fearful.[10]

Modern disciples of Graham look for hidden value in additional ways, but still probe the question "What is this company actually worth?" Buffett modifies the Graham formula by looking at the quality of the business itself. Apostles also use the amount of cashflow generated by the company, the reliability and quality of dividends, and other factors.

- *Verify value by applying the intrinsic value formula.* Graham devised a simple formula to tell if a stock is underpriced. Buy shares only if a company is selling near or below its intrinsic value. The concept has been tested in many different markets and works, though longtime practitioners of value investing say that rigidly following any formula does not produce high returns. This formula takes into account the company's earnings per share (E), its expected earnings growth rate (R), and the current yield on AAA corporate bonds (Y).

The intrinsic value of a stock equals:

$$E(2R + 8.5) \times 4.4/Y$$

- *A pocket calculator is enough.* Graham, who loved mathematics, said so himself:

In 44 years of Wall Street experience and study I have never seen dependable calculations made about common stock values, or related investment policies, that went beyond simple arithmetic or the most elementary algebra. Whenever excalculus is brought in, or higher algebra, you could take it as a warning signal that the operator was trying to substitute theory for experience, and usually also to give speculation the deceptive guise of investment.[11]

- *Relax.* Realize you are unlikely to hit the precise "intrinsic value" of a stock or a stock market right on the mark. A margin of safety will provide peace of mind.
- *Skulk around corporate numbers.* It is a company's future earnings that drive its share price higher, but investors must be wary of estimates that are based on current numbers. Though regulations are tighter now than they were when Graham was investing, earnings

still can be manipulated by creative accountancy. An investor is urged to pay special attention to reserves, accounting changes, and footnotes when reading company documents.

As for estimates of future earnings, anything from false expectations to unexpected world events can repaint the picture. Nevertheless, an investor has to do the best evaluation possible, then make investment choices based on the results.

GRAHAM ON DIVERSIFICATION

Graham's first rule of diversification calls for a distinction between stocks and bonds or bond equivalents. At all times the investor should have a minimum of 25 percent in common stocks and a minimum of 25 percent in securities with a guaranteed rate of return. The remaining 50 percent can be divided between the two categories, depending on which offers the best return.[12]

As a rule of thumb, an investor should back away from the stock market when the earnings per share on leading indices (such as the Dow Jones Industrial Average or the Standard & Poor's Composite Index) is less than the yield on high-quality bonds. When the reverse is true, lean toward bonds.

Graham's second rule of diversification requires the value investor to have a sufficient number of securities in his portfolio, if necessary, with a relatively small number of shares of each stock. While investors like Buffett may have fewer than a dozen or so carefully chosen key companies, Graham usually held 75 or more. Typically, a portfolio can hold from 5 to 30 different issues. The higher the quality of the stocks, the fewer issues are necessary. The least expensive way for an individual investor to buy odd lots is through a company's dividend reinvestment program (DRP).

- *Quality is insurance.* There are two mistakes investors most commonly make. Either they buy poor-quality stocks that will never perform well, or they buy good-quality stocks that are overvalued. Companies with good earnings, a solid dividend history, low debt, and a reasonable price-to-earnings ratio serve best.[13]

- *Bank on the dividends.* A long record of paying dividends, as long as 20 years, shows that a company has substance and is a limited risk.

Chancy growth stocks seldom pay dividends. Furthermore, Graham contended that a niggardly dividend policy harms investors in two ways. Not only are shareholders deprived of income from their investment, but when comparable companies are studied, the one with the lower dividend consistently sells for a lower share price:

> I believe that Wall Street experience shows clearly that the best treatment for stockholders is the payment to them of fair and reasonable dividends in relation to the company's earnings and in relation to the true value of the security, as measured by any ordinary tests based on earning power or assets.[14]

- *Speak out.* No matter what Congress says, shareholders do have rights. If you object to a dividend policy, executive compensation package or merger proposal, organize a shareholder's offensive:

> I want to say a word about disgruntled shareholders. In my humble opinion, not enough of them are disgruntled. And one of the great troubles with Wall Street is that it cannot distinguish between a mere trouble-maker or "strike-suitor" in corporate affairs and a stockholder with a legitimate complaint which deserves attention from his management and from his fellow stockholders.[15]

- *Patience pays off.* An investor subverts progress by focusing on quarterly or even yearly results. It can take a full business cycle—3 to 5 years—for a stock to reach its full value. Only abandon the stock earlier if fundamentals change or if some other factor makes it clear that the stock is going nowhere.[16]

- *Be a contrarian.* Don't follow the crowd. Graham listed two requirements for success on Wall Street: thinking *correctly* and thinking *independently*.[17] By Graham's own example, investors must keep an open mind and continue to search for better ways to ensure safety and maximize growth. *Don't ever stop thinking.*

PARTING WORDS

It is not uncommon for professional value investors to continue investing successfully well into their eighties and nineties. Four notable grand old men of value investing are professional money managers: Roger Murray, Phil Carret, Irving Kahn, and a well-known private investor who was once a client of Benjamin Graham, Robert Heilbrunn. Roger Murray was coauthor of the fifth edition of *Security Analysis*. In 1994 he spoke to students in a value investing seminar at Columbia University. "Through the years," he said, "we've been through every conceivable kind of market. Yet value investing remains a fruitful, useful, and productive discipline."[18]

One last admonition. Enjoy your investing experience. Buying and selling securities and creating a solid portfolio are exciting and challenging endeavors. The markets are ever changing as new stories and new situations continually evolve. Investing can be a lifelong subject of interest, and if addressed with knowledge and "the right attitude," a source of great pleasure.

And though Graham wasn't a gambling man, being a gracious person, he surely would wish every investor the very best of luck.

APPENDIX

GEICO SAGA IS A LESSON FOR "BUY AND HOLD" INVESTORS

One Saturday in 1951, when he was a lanky, crew-cut graduate student at Columbia University, Warren Buffett caught a train to Washington, made his way to the headquarters of Government Employees Insurance Co., then wandered around the locked building looking for someone to talk to. Finally he saw a janitor inside and tapped on the window. The janitor told the 20-year-old that there was a guy upstairs who might be able to answer questions for him.

The man upstairs was Lorimer A. Davidson, Geico president and later chief executive. Davidson spent most of that Saturday educating young Buffett on the economics of the insurance industry. That was the beginning of a story that reached its denouement in 1995 when Buffett's company, Berkshire Hathaway Inc., made a $2.3 billion, or $70 per share, offer to buy the 49 percent of Geico it didn't already own.

"On a personal note, I would like to thank Lorimer A. Davidson, former CEO of Geico, for first opening my eyes to the potential for Geico some 44 years ago," Buffett said in the press release announcing the acquisition offer. Davidson is now 91 years old.

The story of Geico and Buffett is a double American Horatio Alger story. Both show how good ideas and an indomitable spirit can still lead to success in America.

Geico was the first subject that Buffett, who each year ranks as either first or second wealthiest man in the United States, incorporated into what he calls his "circle of competence." Buffett will not invest in businesses that he does not thoroughly understand.

Not only does Buffett understand insurance, his association with Geico has been more than merely business. Buffett made the trip to Geico headquarters in 1951 because he'd discovered that his investment professor, Benjamin Graham, was a director of the company. Buffett needed a stock to study as a class project, and he felt he might get the best lesson from Geico, since Graham obviously knew so much about it.

Graham, who became Buffett's mentor, in fact owned 48 percent of the company and was responsible for taking Geico public in 1949. Geico was among the most successful initial public offerings on Wall Street ever. Since then Geico, the holding company for Government Employees Insurance Co. and several other subsidiaries, has become one of the nation's largest auto insurers.

Geico was started during the Great Depression by Leo Goodwin, an accountant for a Texas insurer, who believed he could make a successful business by selling to low-risk government employees without agencies. In 1936, at age 50, Goodwin founded Geico with $100,000. Cleaves Rhea, a Fort Worth banker, put up 75 percent of the money. Goodwin and his wife, Lillian, worked 12 hours a day for a combined income of $250 per month to get the business started. The following year they moved it to Washington, D.C., to be near a larger client base. By 1940 the company was profitable.

In 1948, however, the Rhea family wanted to sell its interest in the company. Geico was shopped around Wall Street with no success until representatives called on the Graham Newman Co. and talked to Graham.

Graham looked at Geico and recognized its value immediately, though the company did carry some risk. Graham had some concern that the company's assets were not as strong as he would have liked. Also, the investment required nearly 25 percent of Graham Newman's assets. Graham, an ultraconservative with a lifelong record of more than 17 percent average annual return (including the depression years), had never before put that much of his money in a single investment.

Walter Schloss, who worked for Graham at the time and now is an extremely successful money manager, recalls Graham's angst. "Walter," Graham said to Schloss, "if this purchase doesn't work out, we can always liquidate it and get our money back."

Graham paid $720,000 for the same percentage of Geico for which Buffett in 1995 paid $2.3 billion. Graham's purchase triggered a dramatic series of events. First of all, the Securities and Exchange Commission immediately demanded that Graham Newman cancel the sale, since at that time an investment company could not own more than 10 percent of an insurance company.

The sellers, however, would not take Geico back. Instead, Graham negotiated an agreement with the SEC whereby he would spin off Geico and distribute the shares to investors in the Graham Newman Fund.

When Geico began trading on the New York Stock Exchange, investor reaction was remarkable. Geico went public at $27 per share. The company spun off some subsidiaries to shareholders, then underwent several stock splits; it was estimated that between 1948 and 1972 the shares appreciated more than 28,000 percent.

However, the company's progress wasn't smooth. Both Graham and his partner, Jerry Newman, were Geico board members, but in the early 1970s they decided to retire. Newman nominated Warren Buffett to replace him on the board, and Graham wrote a letter to other board members backing the recommendation. The board rejected Buffett's name because of the possibility of conflicts of interest. Buffett, who had worked for Graham Newman until the company dissolved, was operating a fund from Omaha. His fund had investments in other insurance companies as well.

The board might have saved itself a lot of grief if it had found a way for Buffett to serve. In 1973 Geico shares were trading at about $60; by mid-1976 the priced had declined to $5. By then Geico was on the verge of bankruptcy and Leo and Lillian Goodwin's son, who was then running the company, committed suicide.

Buffett had purchased $7000 worth of shares, investing 65 percent of his net worth, shortly after his 1951 visit to Geico. He sold the shares at the market peak. In 1976 Buffett again invested in Geico, buying 1.3 million shares at an average cost of $3.18 per share. Gradually over the following years, Buffett increased his ownership until it reached 51 percent.

When the acquisition was completed in 1996, Buffett bought back some of the original shares owned by Graham heirs. Graham's grandson recently financed his medical school education by selling some inherited stock. This year a grandniece of Graham's discovered she owned a block of Geico shares that were given to her by her grandmother, although registered in a misspelled name.

Buffett still does not serve on the Geico board. However, William Ruane, founder of the Sequoia Fund and a close friend and classmate of Buffett's in Graham's course at Columbia, does. In the circular path of the investment world, the Sequoia Fund also is a major Berkshire Hathaway shareholder.

The insurance business plays a key role in Berkshire Hathaway's success. Insurance operations account for 85 percent of Berkshire's $21.3 billion in assets. It is through the investment portfolios of the insurance holdings that Berkshire owns its Geico stake, plus its holdings in Coca Cola Co., Gillette Co., Washington Post Co., and one of Buffett's occasional clunkers, Salomon Inc. An array of other companies, including the Buffalo News, Nebraska Furniture Mart, and See's Candy, are held outside the insurance group.

All this may imply that Buffett's investment in Geico is primarily sentimental in nature—that he is fulfilling a youthful dream of owning Geico. He often has said that Graham had more influence on him than any other person, with the exception of Buffett's father. Is it a present to Buffett from himself to decisively best his old master by owning the company that was Graham's crowning achievement? Buffett will be 65 soon.

It is unlikely that Buffett's investment has a psychological motivation, since competing with Graham was like competing with someone who wasn't seriously playing the game. Though Graham was a master investor, Buffett himself says that Graham was a professorial type whose interest was based more on the intellectual challenge than on acquisitiveness. Neither Graham nor Buffett seems driven by greed. In any case, Buffett's record left Graham's in the dust many years ago.

Perhaps Buffett is allocating an amount equal to the $2 billion Berkshire will receive from its share of the sale of Cap Cities/ABC to the Walt Disney Co. to Geico simply because it is a good investment. Geico's total assets are almost $5 billion, so Buffett is buying the company for somewhat less than its asset value. Though the company recently went through some restructuring to get out of the homeowner's insurance business (it was hit hard by the 1994 Los Angeles earthquake), it still has a healthy 14 percent return on equity. In choosing investments, Buffett says he's more interested in return on equity than on assets, preferring companies whose future ROE seems brighter than today's.

Buffett may have had another motive for buying the remainder of Geico. Maybe he limited his investments to companies he already controls out of kindness to the rest of the investment world. At the 1995 Berkshire annual meeting Buffett explained the difficulties of reinvesting his company's tremendous profits, which have averaged 23 percent annual return on shareholders' equity since 1965.

"If we grew at the same rate, assuming we paid no dividends, we would gobble up the whole GDP in a period that would not take that long," Buffett said.

This appendix first appeared as an article written by Janet Lowe and distributed by Knight-Ridder Financial News Service in September 1995.

 NOTES

NOTES: CHAPTER 1

1. Warren Buffett, remarks at the 1995 Berkshire Hathaway annual meeting.

2. "Three Simple Methods of Common Stock Selection," 1975 speech by Benjamin Graham.

3. James Grant, *Minding Mr. Market: Ten Years on Wall Street with Grant's Interest Rate Observer* (New York: Farrar Straus Giroux, 1993), p. 281. Copyright © 1993 by James Grant. Reprinted by permission of Farrar, Straus, & Giroux, Inc.

4. Ibid., p. 283.

5. Andrew Bary, *Barron's*, March 13, 1995, p. 28.

6. Warren Buffett, "Benjamin Graham," *Financial Analysts Journal*, November–December 1976.

7. Benjamin Graham, *The Intelligent Investor* (New York: Harper & Row, 1949), pp. 204–205. Reprinted by permission of HarperCollins Publishers, Inc.

8. John Train, *The Money Masters* (New York: Harper & Row, 1985), p. 228.

9. Benjamin Graham, "Renaissance of Value," *Barron's*, September 23, 1974. Reprinted by permission of Dow Jones & Company, Inc. All rights reserved worldwide.

10. Berkshire Hathaway 1994 annual report, p. 5. Copyrighted material is reproduced with the permission of Warren Buffett.

11. George W. Bishop, Jr., *Charles H. Dow and the Dow Theory* (New York: Appleton-Century-Crofts, 1960), p. 121.

12. Benjamin Graham and David Dodd, *Security Analysis* (New York: McGraw Hill, 1940), p. 343. Reproduced with the permission of The McGraw-Hill Companies.

13. Bishop, op. cit., p. 120.

14. Graham and Dodd, op. cit., p. 19.

15. Berkshire Hathaway 1994 annual report, p. 6. Copyrighted material is reproduced with the permission of Warren Buffett.

16. Ibid., p. 10. Copyrighted material is reproduced with the permission of Warren Buffett.

17 Terence P. Paré, "Yes, You Can Beat the Market," *Fortune*, April 3, 1995, p. 69.

18. Peter Lynch, *One Up on Wall Street* (New York: Penguin Books, 1989), p. 156.

NOTES: CHAPTER 2

1. Benjamin Graham and David Dodd, *Security Analysis* (New York: McGraw-Hill, 1940), pp. 20–21. Reproduced with the permission of The McGraw-Hill Companies.

2. Ibid.

3. Ibid., p. 24.

4. Martin Capital Management newsletter, June 1995.

5. Graham and Dodd, op. cit., pp. 432–433.

6. Terence P. Paré, "Yes, You Can Beat the Market," *Fortune*, April 3, 1995, p. 70.

7. Andrew Bary, "The Last Disciple," *Barron's*, March 13, 1995, p. 28.

8. Benjamin Graham, *The Intelligent Investor* (New York: Harper & Brothers, 1954), p. 249. Reprinted by permission of HarperCollins Publishers, Inc.

9. Graham and Dodd, op. cit., p. 402.

10. Benjamin Graham and Charles McGolrick, *The Interpretation of Financial Statements* (New York: Harper & Brothers, 1937), p. 20.

11. John Downes and Jordan Elliot Goodman, *Dictionary of Finance and Investment Terms* (New York: Barron's Educational Series, 1991), pp. 30–31.

12. Peter Lynch, *One Up on Wall Street* (New York: Penguin Books, 1989), p. 115.

13. Warren Buffett, 1994 Berkshire Hathaway letters to shareholders, p. 68. Copyrighted material is reproduced with the permission of Warren Buffett.

14. Graham and Dodd, op. cit., p. 577.

15. Warren Buffett, 1995 Berkshire Hathaway annual meeting.

16. John Dorfman, "Heard on the Street," *The Wall Street Journal,* December 7, 1994, p. C-2.

17. Graham and Dodd, op. cit., pp. 576–577.

18. Ibid., p. 577.

19. Lynch, op. cit., p. 235.

20. Graham and Dodd, op. cit., p. 543.

21. Warren Buffett, 1987 Berkshire Hathaway annual report.

22. Graham and Dodd, op. cit., p. 590.

23. James Grant, *Minding Mr. Market* (New York: Farrar Straus Giroux, 1993), p. 251. Reprinted by permission of Farrar, Straus & Giroux, Inc.

24. Graham and Dodd, op. cit., p. 579.

25. Ibid., p. 583.

26. Ibid.

27. Ibid., p. 375.

28. Benjamin Graham, *Current Problems in Security Analysis* (Transcripts of Lectures, September 1946–February 1947), p. 128.

29. George W. Bishop, Jr., *Charles H. Dow and the Dow Theory* (New York: Appleton-Century-Crofts, 1960), p. 52.

NOTES: CHAPTER 3

1. Peter Lynch, *One Up on Wall Street* (New York: Penguin Books, 1989), p. 218.

2. Benjamin Graham and David Dodd, *Security Analysis* (New York: McGraw-Hill, 1940), p. 608. Reproduced with the permission of The McGraw-Hill Companies.

3. Charles Munger, comments at 1995 Berkshire Hathaway annual meeting.

4. Lynch, op. cit., p. 220.

5. Charles Brandes, *Value Investing Today* (Homewood, IL: Dow Jones-Irwin, 1989), p. 79.

6. Benjamin Graham, *The Intelligent Investor* (New York: Harper & Row, 1973), p. 178. Reprinted by permission of HarperCollins Publishers, Inc.

7. Benjamin Graham, quoted in *Financial Analysts Journal*, September–October, 1976.

8. Statement to author, January 1995.

9. Graham and Dodd, op. cit., p. 531.

10. Ibid., p. 532.

11. Ibid., p. 561.

12. Ibid., p. 510.

13. Ibid., p. 41.

14. Comments at 1995 Berkshire Hathaway annual meeting.

15. Lynch, op. cit., p. 169.

16. Frank Lalli, "Wise Words and What to Buy, When to Sell," *Money*, June 1994, p. 7.

17. Graham and Dodd, op. cit., p. 364.

18. Ibid, p. 686.

19. Lynch, op. cit., p. 152.

20. Irving Kahn and Robert D. Milne, *Benjamin Graham: The Father of Financial Analysis* (Charlottesville, VA: Financial Analysts Research Foundation, 1977), p. 37.

21. Comments at 1995 Berkshire Hathaway annual meeting.

22. Graham and Dodd, op. cit., p. 508.

NOTES: CHAPTER 4

1. Benjamin Graham and David Dodd, *Security Analysis* (New York: McGraw-Hill, 1940), p. 609. Reproduced with the permission of The McGraw-Hill Companies.

2. Ibid., p. 597.

3. Warren Buffett, 1995 Berkshire Hathaway annual meeting.

4. Ibid.

5. Ibid.

6. Charles Brandes, *Value Investing Today* (Homewood, IL: Dow Jones-Irwin, 1989), p. 41.

7. 1994 Berkshire Hathaway annual report to shareholders, p. 2. Copyrighted material is reproduced with the permission of Warren Buffett.

8. Brandes, op. cit., p. 40.

9. Graham and Dodd, op. cit., p. 40.

10. Brandes, op. cit., p. 81.

11. Benjamin Graham, *The Intelligent Investor* (New York: Harper & Row, 1949), p.110. Reprinted by permission of HarperCollins Publishers, Inc.

12. Graham and Dodd, op. cit., p. 601.

13. Brandes, op. cit., p. 31.

14. Andrew Bary, *Barron's*, March 13, 1995.

15. Graham and Dodd, op. cit., p. 594.

16. Ibid.

17. Ibid., Ch. 44, p. 12.

NOTES: CHAPTER 5

1. Benjamin Graham, *The Intelligent Investor* (New York: Harper & Row, 1973), p. 40. Reprinted by permission of HarperCollins Publishers, Inc.

2. Warren Buffett, message to Buffett Limited Partnership, 1965.

3. George W. Bishop, Jr., *Charles H. Dow and the Dow Theory* (New York: Appleton-Century-Crofts, 1960), p. 69.

4. National Association of Investment Corporations Investors Manual, Royal Oak, MI, 1989, p.16.

5. Graham, op. cit., p.106. Reprinted by permission of HarperCollins Publishers, Inc.

6. Frank Lalli, "The Money Men," *Forbes*, January 1, 1972, p. 89.

7. Warren Buffett, comments at the 1995 Berkshire Hathaway annual meeting.

8. Graham, op. cit., p. 54. Reprinted by permission of HarperCollins Publishers, Inc.

9. Benjamin Graham, "The Simplest Way to Select Bargain Stocks," Special Report, *Medical Economics*, September 20, 1976.

10. Charles H. Brandes, *Value Investing Today* (Homewood, IL: Dow Jones-Irwin, 1989), p. 132.

11. Warren Buffett, comments at the 1995 Berkshire Hathaway annual meeting.

12. Brandes International Fund Prospectus, San Diego, 1995.

13. Graham, *Medical Economics.*

14. Warren Buffett, comments, at the 1994 Berkshire Hathaway annual meeting.

15. Benjamin Graham and David Dodd, *Security Analysis* (New York: McGraw-Hill, 1940), p. 681. Reprinted by permission of The McGraw-Hill Companies.

16. Janet Lowe, *Benjamin Graham on Value Investing* (Chicago: Dearborn Financial Publishing, 1994), p. 175.

17. Bishop, op. cit., p. 48.

18. Warren Buffett, Berkshire Hathaway 1994 annual report, p. 6. Copyrighted material is reproduced with the permission of Warren Buffett.

NOTES: CHAPTER 6

1. From an interview with Marjorie Graham Janis, 1993.

2. Catherine Davidson, "Graham and Dodd's *Security Analysis: The Fifth Edition,*" *Hermes,* Fall 1987.

3. Benjamin Graham and David Dodd, *Security Analysis* (New York: McGraw-Hill, 1940), p. 557. Reprinted by permission of The McGraw-Hill Companies.

4. Ibid.

5. Davidson, op. cit., p. 30.

6. Graham and Dodd, op. cit., p. 369.

7. Janet Lowe, *Benjamin Graham on Value Investing* (Chicago: Dearborn Financial Publishing, 1994), p. 218.

8. Warren Buffett, letter to partners, October 9, 1967. Copyrighted material is reproduced with the permission of Warren Buffett.

9. Graham and Dodd, op. cit., p. 36.

10. Ibid., p. 691.

11. David Dreman, "An Inefficient Hypothesis," *Forbes,* April 26, 1993, p. 402. Reprinted by permission of *Forbes* Magazine © Forbes Inc., 1994.

12. Warren Buffett, comments at 1995 Berkshire Hathaway annual meeting.

13. Charles Brandes, *Value Investing Today* (Homewood, IL: Dow Jones-Irwin, 1989), p. 39.

14. Peter Lynch, *One Up on Wall Street* (New York: Penguin Books, 1989), p. 136.

15. Ibid., p. 139.

16. Benjamin Graham, *The Intelligent Investor* (New York: Harper & Row, 1973), pp. 183–200. Reprinted by permission of HarperCollins Publishers, Inc.

17. "Three Simple Methods of Common Stock Selection," 1975 speech by Benjamin Graham.

18. Ibid.

19. Arthur H. Medalic, *Value Line*, May 26, 1995.

20. Graham and Dodd, op. cit., p. 594.

21. Benjamin Graham, "Current Problems in Security Analysis" (Transcripts of Lectures, September 1946–February 1947), p. 146.

22. Brandes, op. cit., p. 32.

23. Graham and Dodd, op. cit., p. 720.

24. Ibid., p. 555.

NOTES: CHAPTER 7

1. James Grant, *Minding Mr. Market* (New York: Farrar Straus Giroux, 1993), p. xv. Reprinted by permission of Farrar, Straus & Giroux, Inc.

2. Sequoia Fund 1987 third quarter report.

3. Berkshire Hathaway letters to shareholders, 1989–1990, p. 6.

4. Ibid.

5. Benjamin Graham, *The Intelligent Investor* (New York: Harper & Brothers, 1954), p. 109. Reprinted by permission of HarperCollins Publishers, Inc.

6. Graham and Dodd, *Security Analysis* (New York: McGraw-Hill, 1940), p. 25. Reprinted by permission of The McGraw-Hill Companies.

7. Ibid., p. 720.

8. Graham, op. cit., p. 97.

9. George W. Bishop, Jr., *Charles Dow and the Dow theory* (New York: Appleton-Century-Crofts, 1960), p. 60.

10. Ibid., p. 106.

11. Ibid., p. 138.

12. John R. Graham, University of Utah, Salt Lake City and Campbell R. Harvey, Duke University, Durham, NC.

13. John Train, *The Money Masters* (New York: Harper & Row, 1985), p. 85.

14. Benjamin Graham, "Inflated Treasuries and Deflated Stockholders," *Forbes*, June 1, 1932, p. 10.

15. Benjamin Graham, "Renaissance of Value," *Barron's*, September 23, 1974. Reprinted by permission of Dow Jones & Company, Inc. All rights reserved worldwide.

16. Seth Klarman, *Margin of Safety* (New York: Harper Business, 1991), p. xix.

17. Charles Brandes, *Value Investing Today* (Homewood, IL: Dow Jones-Irwin, 1989), p. 100.

18. Graham, *Intelligent Investor*, p. 369. Reprinted by permission of Harper-Collins Publishers, Inc.

19. Ibid., p. 13. Reprinted by permission of HarperCollins Publishers, Inc.

20. Graham and Dodd, op. cit., p. 27.

21. Graham and Dodd, op. cit., p. 25.

22. Klarman, op. cit., p. 11.

NOTES: CHAPTER 8

1. Benjamin Graham, *The Intelligent Investor* (New York: Harper & Row, 1973), p. 98. Reprinted by permission of HarperCollins Publishers, Inc.

2. David Dreman, "An Inefficient Hypothesis," *Forbes*, April 26, 1993, p. 402.

3. Ibid.

4. David Dreman, "An Inefficient Hypothesis," *Forbes*, March 3, 1994, p. 146.

5. Charles Brandes, *Value Investing Today* (Homewood, IL: Dow Jones-Irwin, 1989), p. 79.

6. Roger Lowenstein, "Where's the Reward in Hedging Against Risk?" *The Wall Street Journal*, April 27, 1995, p. C1.

7. Peter Lynch, *One Up on Wall Street* (New York: Penguin Books, 1989), p. 280.

8. Peter L. Bernstein, "Risk as a History of Ideas," *Financial Analysts Journal*, January–February 1995.

9. Lynch, op. cit., p. 280.

10. Warren Buffett, comments at 1995 Berkshire Hathaway annual meeting.

11. Benjamin Graham and David Dodd, *Security Analysis* (New York: McGraw-Hill, 1940), p. 17.

12. Seth A. Klarman, *Margin of Safety: Risk-Averse Value Investing Strategies for the Thoughtful Investor* (New York: Harper Business, 1991), p. 8.

13. Graham and Dodd, op. cit., p. 29.

14. Warren Buffett, 1968 Berkshire Hathaway letters to partners.

15. James Grant, *Minding Mr. Market* (New York: Farrar Straus Giroux, 1993), p. xiv. Reprinted by permission of Farrar, Straus & Giroux, Inc.

16. Graham and Dodd, op. cit., p. 661.

17. Ibid., p. x.

NOTES: CHAPTER 9

1. James Grant, *Minding Mr. Market* (New York: Farrar Straus Giroux, 1993), p. xv. Reprinted by permission of Farrar, Straus & Giroux, Inc.

2. Benjamin Graham, *The Intelligent Investor* (New York: Harper & Row, 1975), p. 289. Reprinted by permission of HarperCollins Publishers, Inc.

3. Ibid. Reprinted by permission of HarperCollins Publishers, Inc.

4. Warren Buffett, letter to Buffett Limited Partnership, 1963.

5. Benjamin Graham and David Dodd, *Security Analysis* (New York: McGraw-Hill, 1940), p. x.

6. "Efficiency and After," *The Economist*, October 9, 1993, p. 4.

7. Ibid.

8. Irving Kahn and Robert D. Milne, *Benjamin Graham: The Father of Financial Analysis* (Charlottesville, VA: Financial Analysts Research Association, 1977).

9. Andrew Kilpatrick, *Of Permanent Value* (Birmingham, AL: AKPE, 1994), pp. 288–289.

10. "Beware the IPO Market," *Business Week*, April 4, 1994.

11. Peter Lynch, "IPOs Explained," *Worth*, February 16, 1993.

12. Graham and Dodd, op. cit., p. 657.

13. Grant, op. cit., p. xiv. Reprinted by permission of Farrar, Straus & Giroux, Inc.

14. Warren Buffett, comments at 1995 Berkshire Hathaway annual meeting.

NOTES: CHAPTER 10

1. Andrew Weiss, "The Guru of Value Investing Takes a Long View," *Hermes*, Fall 1994, p. 17.

2. Warren Buffett, 1995 Berkshire Hathaway annual meeting.

3. Irving Kahn and Robert D. Milne, *Benjamin Graham: The Father of Financial Analysis* (Charlottesville, VA: Financial Analysts Research Foundation, 1976).

4. Charles Brandes, *Value Investing Today* (Homewood, IL: Dow Jones-Irwin, 1989) p. 1.

5. Kahn and Milne, op. cit., p. 37.

6. Extracted from Hearings Before the Committee on Banking and Currency, U.S. Senate, 84th Congress, U.S. Government Printing Office, March 11, 1955, p. 546.

7. Frank Lalli, "Wise Words on What to Buy, When to Sell," *Money*, June 1994, p. 7.

8. Warren Buffett, comments at 1995 Berkshire Hathaway annual meeting.

9. Ibid.

10. Benjamin Graham, "Current Problems in Security Analysis" Transcripts of Lectures, September 1946–February 1947, p. 48.

11. Benjamin Graham, "The New Speculation in Common Stocks," *The Analysts Journal,* June 1958, pp. 17–21.

12. Frank Lalli, "The Money Men," *Forbes*, January 1, 1972, p. 89.

13. Graham, "Current Problems in Security Analysis," p. 96.

14. Ibid., p. 128.

15. Ibid., p. 102.

16. "The Simplest Way to Select Bargain Stocks," Special Report, *Medical Economics,* September 20, 1976.

17. Kahn and Milne, op. cit., p. 41.

18. Weiss, op. cit.

GLOSSARY

American depositary receipt (ADR) A way U.S. citizens can buy and sell publicly traded companies in foreign countries. The receipt shows that shares of a foreign corporation are held on deposit or under control of a U.S. banking institution. The bank acts as the transfer agent and collects dividends on behalf of the owner.

Asset allocation The assignment of investment funds to specific categories of securities—utility shares, U.S. industrial stocks, foreign stocks, bonds, and so forth. Studies show that if an investor can anticipate the best category to be in during a specific period, investment returns are significantly higher.

Balance sheet A financial statement showing a company's assets, liabilities, and capital on a specific date.

Bear market According to stock market lore, a bear turns and runs when confronted, though certain national park visitors might take exception to that notion. A bear market, nevertheless, is in retreat and is declining.

Book value Total assets *minus* intangible assets *minus* liabilities *minus* stock issues ahead of common stock. To get book value per share, *divide* by the number of shares outstanding. Book value of an issue such as preferred or secondary preferred is figured by subtracting all issues that take precedence over it, then dividing by the number of share outstanding.

Bull market Bulls charge ahead aggressively, and so does a bull market. A bull market is on the rise.

Business cycle movements   Movements in the stock markets, or within categories of stocks, as a result of predictable business cycles. For example, there is an established automobile-buying cycle, a cycle for small appliances, and a durable-goods cycle. These cycles can have a profound effect on stock prices.

Call   Technically termed a call option, a call gives the buyer the right to buy a specific number of shares at a specific price by a fixed date. It is the opposite of a **put**.

Capital gain (loss)   Profit or loss from the sale of a capital asset. Short-term capital gains are those realized in less than 6 months. The tax rate for such gains is at a lower rate than that for ordinary income.

Capitalization   The total value of various securities issued by a corporation.

Cash   In corporate accounting, the category is comprised of cash, marketable securities, and any asset that may be used to temporarily stash money.

Cashflow   A company's net income (after taxes) plus the amounts written off for depreciation, depletion, amortization, and other charges.

Common stock   A unit of ownership in a company. Owners of common stock receive dividends after preferred stock. Their claim to assets is junior to all other types of stock in the event of liquidation.

Confirmation of Dow Jones signals   When either the Dow Jones Industrial Average or Transportation Average moves into new high or low ground, the other average must do likewise for the movement to indicate a meaningful trend. Either average may penetrate first.

Contrarian   An investor who does the opposite of what most investors are doing. Contrarians believe that if everyone believes something will happen, it won't. This is because when people believe in an event—that the DJIA is about to plunge, for example—they all take corrective action, which prevents the actual event from occurring. When people believe a stock is going up, they buy the stock, which drives the price up. Contrarians believe they get in before the price rise by looking at securities that others ignore.

Current asset   Cash or something of value that can be converted into cash within 1 year.

Current liability   An obligation due for payment within 1 year.

Current ratio   The current assets divided by the current liabilities. Though requirements vary from one industry to the next, most analysts like companies to have a current ratio of at least 2 to 1, or twice as many current assets as current liabilities.

Derivatives   Any financial instrument in which the return is linked to, or derived from, the performance of some underlying asset such as bonds or currencies or commodities. Futures and options are the commonest forms of derivatives. The more exotic derivatives have catchy names such as inverse floater, swap, cap, and collar.

Dilution   A reduction in the percentage of ownership of the common stockholder by the issuance of additional common shares for less than the current market price.

Diversification   Spreading investment risk by buying different stocks in different industries, or by buying bonds, government securities, money market shares, or the like.

Dividend   A distribution of the earnings of a company to shareholders. Dividend payments are not required except on certain classes of stock, and common stock dividends can vary. The amount is determined each year by the board of directors. Most often dividends are paid in cash, but they can be paid in additional shares of stock, scrip, company products, or property.

Dividend rate   The amount of annual dividend paid per share.

Dividend yield   The ratio of dividend paid to the market price. A stock selling for $100 and paying a dividend of $5 has a dividend yield of 5 percent. Also sometimes called dividend ratio or dividend return.

Dollar cost averaging   Buying a specific dollar amount of a stock each month, regardless of price. This way an investor buys more shares when the price is low and fewer shares when the price is high. The buyer also pays a lower than average price for the shares, since there is never the risk of buying too many shares at too high a price.

Double bottom   When a stock declines, reaches a cyclical low, rallies, then declines again to at or near the earlier low price. If the second decline stops near, but not below the first low point, Charles Dow noted that the subsequent rally could well be the beginning of a strong upward movement.

Double top As a stock advances, the price may suddenly suffer a reversal. If it once again advances to its former high (or very near to it) and declines again, it is said to have seen a double top. Charles Dow observed that a decline from the second top is likely to be severe.

Dow Jones averages Three different market averages computed by the Dow Jones company. They are the Dow Jones Industrial Average of 30 stocks, the Dow Jones Utility Average of 15 public utilities, and the Dow Jones Transportation Average of 20 transportation stocks. The Dow Jones Composite Index includes all 65 stocks. *The Wall Street Journal* prints the list of stocks included in the averages each Monday, and they also can be found in other investment publications.

Dow theory Today the term generally applies to a theory of Charles H. Dow, formulated early in this century. While Dow put forth many insightful theories regarding the stock market and was a creator of the Dow Jones stock market averages, the Dow theory is used in reference to the observation that before a market trend is "confirmed," both the Dow Jones Industrial Average and the Dow Jones Transportation Averages must reach new highs or lows. The interpretations most commonly followed today are those of William Peter Hamilton, who became editor of *The Wall Street Journal* several years after Dow's death.

Earnings per share A company's net income (after taxes) divided by the number of common shares outstanding.

Earnings rate The amount of annual earnings per share, expressed in dollars.

Earnings yield The ratio of annual earnings to market price. A stock earning $5 and selling at $50 has an earnings yield of 10 percent. Sometimes called the price-to-earnings ratio.

Enterprise value The value of a company as an ongoing business enterprise. What is its economic worth to its owners?

Fixed assets An accounting term referring to lands, buildings, equipment, and furnishings.

Fundamental analysis A philosophy whereby stocks are regarded as fractional ownership of the underlying business that they represent.

Goodwill An accounting term referring to the difference between the value of assets and the price paid for them. It also refers to a value placed on the company's reputation, patents, trademarks, location, and other qualities that give the company a competitive advantage.

Income statement   Also called the earnings report or the profit and loss (P&L) statement. It reflects revenues and expenses over an accounting period, usually one quarter or one year.

Intangibles   An accounting term referring to difficult-to-measure assets such as goodwill, brands and trademarks, leaseholds, and reputation. Though intangibles can easily be overstated by companies, they can have enormous worth. The Coca Cola brand name is an example of a highly valuable intangible.

Intrinsic value   The fundamental value of a company based on its ability to produce profits, or its true worth to its owners, as opposed to the company's share price or perceived value.

Junior security   Security with lower priority to claim a company's assets and income. Common stock is subordinate to debt issues and preferred stock, for example.

Leverage   The use of debt to increase buying power.

Liquidation value   The cash a company would amass if it sold all its assets and paid off all its liabilities.

Margin   The buying of securities on credit.

Margin call   An order by a brokerage firm for the investor to pay off an outstanding loan. This could mean the investor has to sell the security that secures the loan.

Margin of safety   The concept that potential investments should be evaluated so as to leave a margin for error. Elements in the selection of a stock or bond or creation of a portfolio should be such as to protect against mistakes or unexpected developments, in much the same way an engineer designs a bridge to bear a heavier weight than ever would be expected. There are various theories on how to achieve a margin of safety.

Multiple   A synonym for the price-to-earnings ratio, or P/E.

Net current asset value   The difference between current assets and current liabilities.

Net income   The income for a company after deducting all expenses.

Net net   Assets *minus* current liabilities *minus* long-term debt.

Operating income   Corporate income after deducting all expenses, except taxes, from normal operations.

Overtrading   Buying on a margin basis in larger amounts than is prudent considering the resources of the investor.

Paper profit (loss)   The unrealized amount above or below the purchase price of a security at which it could currently be sold. The profit or loss is still on paper because the investor in fact still owns the security.

Par value   An arbitrary price intended to indicate the initial price of a corporation's shares. This does not necessarily mean that the shares originally went to market at this price.

Portfolio   Total investment holdings.

Price-to-earnings ratio   A calculation showing how much must be paid for $1 of earning The P/E ratio is derived by dividing the share price by the company's previous 12-month per share earnings. For example, if the stock sells at $26 per share and the earnings are $2 per share, the P/E is 13 to 1. The P/E is sometimes called the multiple.

Primary movements (in the stock market)   A substantial upward swing in the market, which will be tempered by a movement in the opposite direction (see **Secondary movements**). Charles H. Dow felt that the magnitude of a primary movement was difficult, if not impossible, to predict in advance.

Profit and loss statement   Frequently called an income statement or P&L, this accounting document is a summary of a company's revenues and expenses during a specific period. Together with the balance sheet, this document sketches a company's full financial picture.

Prospectus   A document giving details about an offer to sell securities and/or mutual funds. The Securities and Exchange Commission, ordinarily, must approve the document for an initial public offering before it is circulated.

Proxy   A document authorizing one person (often company management) to vote the shares of another person (often the shareholder).

Puts   Technically called a put option, this contract gives a seller the right to sell a specific number of shares at a specific price by a certain date. The put option buyer pays the seller a premium for this right. For example, a purchaser of an ABC December 50 put has the right to sell 100 shares of ABC at $50 to the put seller at any time until the contract expires in December. The buyer expects the stock price to fall, while the seller expects the price to remain stable, rise, or drop by an amount less than his or her profit on the premium. This is the opposite of a **call** option.

Qualitative analysis Analysis based on nonnumerical factors, such as market share, location of business, industry group, and name recognition.

Quantitative analysis Analysis based on financial statement numbers.

Secondary movements (in the stock market) According to Charles H. Dow, the law of action and reactions dictates that a primary movement in the market will have a secondary movement in the opposite direction of at least three-eighths of the primary movement. For example, if a stock advances 10 points, it is likely to relapse 4 points. The same rule applies to movements on individual stocks, according to Dow.

Red herring A prospectus for an initial public offering of corporate shares. It is called a red herring because it contains warnings of risk throughout, printed in red.

Retained earnings Corporate net income that has not been distributed to shareholders, but rather is held in corporate coffers for specific or general use.

Return on invested capital Net income plus interest expense divided by total capitalization.

Securities and Exchange Commission (SEC) A U.S. government agency that regulates and supervises the securities industry. It was established in the New Deal of the 1930s.

Securities and Exchange Commission (SEC) documents The SEC requires certain documents to be filed by corporations at specific times. Form 10-K is an annual business and financial report; Form 10-Q is the quarterly financial report; a Form 8-K must be filed within 15 days of unscheduled material events or corporate changes. Additionally, companies must file proxy statements for annual meetings, merger proxy statements in the case of a merger, and a prospectus when securities are to be offered publicly.

Senior security A security that ranks above common stocks in the event of liquidation, such as a bond or a preferred stock.

Short sale   A stock sold, but not yet owned, by an investor. The stock must later be bought for delivery to the source from which it has been borrowed. An investor "sells short" when a share price seems to be declining and he believes he can buy the shares at a lower price later and make a profit.

Split   Dividing the number of outstanding shares into a larger number. The overall percentage of the company owned by the shareholder remains constant.

Total return   Dividends plus capital gains (growth in share price).

Warrant   A type of security, usually issued together with a bond or preferred stock, that entitles the holder to buy a proportionate amount of common stock at a specific price, usually higher than the market price at the time the warrant is issued. Warrants are transferable and are traded on the major exchanges. Also called subscription warrants or stock purchase warrants.

Working capital   The excess of current assets over current liabilities. This is a key measure of company's strength.

Yield   The percentage of cash return on an investor's money. It is the annual dividend divided by the price.

 RECOMMENDED
READING

BOOKS

Baruch, Bernard. *My Own Story*, 1957. No longer available. Look for it in used bookstores and through rare book dealers.

Bishop, George W., Jr. *Charles H. Dow and the Dow Theory*. New York: Appleton-Century-Crofts, 1960. This book is out of print. If you can find it at a used bookstore, as I did, grab it.

Bodie, Zvi, Alex Kane, and Alan J. Marcus. *Investments*, 2nd ed. Homewood, IL: Richard D. Irwin, 1991.

Branch, Ben. *Investments: Principles and Practices*. Chicago: Dearborn Financial Publishing, 1989.

Brandes, Charles H. *Value Investing Today*. Homewood, IL: Dow Jones-Irwin, 1989.

Carret, Philip. *The Art of Speculation*, 1930. This classic book was written by the founder of the Pioneer Fund, who is still actively traveling and investing today though he is more than 90 years old. This rare book can be located through Wall Street Books, P.O. Box 24A06, Los Angeles, CA 90023. Tel. 310-476-6732.

Cohen, Jerome B., Edward D. Zinbarg, and Arthur Zeikel. *Investment Analysis and Portfolio Management*, 5th ed. Homewood, IL: Richard D. Irwin, 1986.

Coulson, D. Robert. *The Intelligent Investor's Guide to Profiting from Stock Market Inefficiencies*. Chicago: Probus Publishing, 1987.

Downes, John, and Jordan Elliot Goodman. *Finance and Investment Handbook*, 4th ed. Hauppauge, NY: Barron's Educational Series, 1995.

Fischer, Donald E., and Ronald J. Jordan. *Security Analysis and Portfolio Management*, 5th ed. Des Moines, IA: Prentice-Hall, 1991.

Fisher, Kenneth. *Super Stocks.* Homewood, IL: Dow Jones-Irwin, 1984.

Fisher, Philip. *Paths to Wealth Through Common Stocks*, 1960. Look for this book through Wall Street Books. See the Phillip Carret entry.

Francis, Jack Clark. *Investments: Analysis and Management*, 5th ed. New York: McGraw-Hill, 1991.

Graham, Benjamin, and David L. Dodd. *Security Analysis*, New York: McGraw-Hill, 1934; 2nd ed., 1940; 3rd ed., 1951; 4th ed. (with Sidney Cottel and Charles Tatham), 1962; 5th ed., (Frank E. Block, Roger F. Murray, and Sydney Cottle), 1988.

Graham, Benjamin, and Charles McGolrick. *The Interpretation of Financial Statements.* New York: Harper & Row, 1937; 2nd ed., 1955. Look for this book in every used bookstore you can find. Simple and easy to read, it illuminates the classic concepts of finance.

Graham, Benjamin. *Storage and Stability: A Modern Ever-Normal Granary.* New York: McGraw-Hill, 1937. There are people who say that if the proposals accepted at Bretton Woods had belonged to Ben Graham rather than John Maynard Keynes, the world would be a peaceful, well-fed place today.

Graham, Benjamin. *World Commodities and World Currency.* New York: McGraw-Hill, 1944. A follow-on to *Storage and Stability*.

Graham, Benjamin. *The Intelligent Investor.* New York: Harper & Row, 1949; 2nd ed., 1954; 3rd ed., 1959; 4th ed., 1973.

Graham, Benjamin (transl.). *The Truce* by Mario Benedetti. New York: Harper & Row, 1967. From the Spanish.

Grant, James. *Minding Mr. Market: Ten Years on Wall Street with Grant's Interest Rate Observer.* New York: Farrar Straus Giroux, 1993. An entertaining look at the stupidity and sagacity of Wall Street.

Hagstrom, Robert G., Jr. *The Warren Buffett Way: Investment Strategies of the World's Greatest Investor.* New York: John Wiley, 1994.

Hirt, Geoffrey A., and Stanley B. Block. *Fundamentals of Investment Management,* 4th ed. Homewood, IL: Richard D. Irwin, 1992.

Kilpatrick, Andrew. *Warren Buffett: The Good Guy of Wall Street.* New York: Donald I. Fine, 1992.

Kilpatrick, Andrew. *Of Permanent Value: The Story of Warren Buffett.* Birmingham, AL: AKPE, 1994.

Klarman, Seth. *Margin of Safety: Risk-Averse Value Investing Strategies for the Thoughtful Investor.* New York: Harper Business, 1991.

Lewis, Michael. *Liar's Poker,* New York: Penguin Books, 1989. Read this for entertainment, but also to remind yourself that the companies we invest in aren't simply abstract pieces of paper called stocks. They are made up of real people doing some outrageous things.

Lowe, Janet. *Benjamin Graham on Value Investing: Lessons from the Dean of Wall Street.* Chicago: Dearborn Financial Publishing, 1994.

Lowe, Janet, *Keys to Investing in International Stocks.* New York: Barron's, 1993.

Lowe, Janet, and Geraldine Weiss. *Dividends Don't Lie: Finding Value in Blue Chip Stocks.* Chicago: Dearborn Financial Publishing, 1989.

Lynch, Peter, with John Rothchild. *One Up on Wall Street: How to Use What You Already Know to Make Money in the Market.* New York: Penguin Books, 1990. The first third of the book is overly basic, but hang in there. Lynch's book is disorganized and often couched in nonsequiturs, but if you pay attention and read the message behind the words, it becomes clear why he made so much money for Fidelity Magellan.

Lynch, Peter, with John Rothchild., *Beating the Street.* New York: Simon & Schuster, 1993.

O'Higgins, Michael, and John Downes. *Beating the Dow,* New York: Harper Perennial, 1992.

Radcliffe, Robert C. *Investment.* Glenview, IL: Harper Collins, 1990.

Reilly, Frank K. *Investment Analysis and Portfolio Management,* 3rd ed. Orlando, FL: Harcourt Brace, 1989.

Rhea, Robert. *The Dow Theory,* 1932. This classic book is no longer in print. Copies may be available through Wall Street Books. For full details, check the listing on Philip Carret.

Smith, Adam. *Supermoney*. New York: Random House, 1972.

Soros, George. *The Alchemy of Finance*. New York: John Wiley, 1987. This is sophisticated stuff. Too risky for the value investor, but fascinating reading.

Train, John. *The Midas Touch*. New York: Harper & Row, 1987. A bit dated and flip in tone, it nonetheless has some good lessons.

Train, John. *The Money Masters*. New York: Harper & Row, 1980.

Train, John. *The New Money Masters*. New York: Harper & Row, 1989. This is "The Midas Touch II."

INVESTMENT DATA RESEARCH SOURCES

Barron's: 200 Liberty St., New York, NY 10281.

The Economist: 111 West 57th St., New York, NY 10019.

The Financial Times: 14 E. 60th St. New York, NY 10126. Daily newspaper published in London. Carries international news and share prices.

Morgan Stanley Inc.: 1633 Broadway, New York, NY 10019. Morgan Stanley capital investment perspective, published quarterly. Price and financial data on 1750 foreign securities.

Standard & Poor's Stock Sheets: Standard & Poor's Corp., 25 Broadway, New York, NY 10004. Financial data in compact form on more than 5300 common and preferred stocks, published monthly.

Value Line Investment Surveys: 711 Third Ave., New York, NY 10017. One-page reports and analysis for 1700 companies. All reports updated each 13 weeks; industries updated weekly.

The Wall Street Journal: subscription address and telephone number: 200 Burnett Rd., Chicopee, MA 01020. Call 1-800-JOURNAL. The foremost financial newspaper worldwide.

INDEX

Other Works in McGraw-Hill's
Benjamin Graham Collection

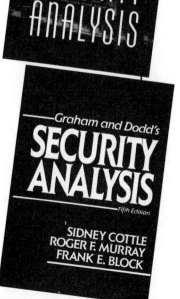